FASHION CROCHET

FASHION CROCHET

Jean Kinmond

B T Batsford Limited   London

Charles T Branford Company   Boston, Massachusetts

© Jean Kinmond 1972
First published 1972
ISBN 0 7134 2653 5
ISBN (USA) 1 8231 5035 6
Library of Congress Catalog card number 72 172615

Set in Monophoto Times New Roman 9 on 10 point
Printed and bound in Great Britain by
William Clowes & Sons, Limited, London, Beccles and Colchester
for the publishers
B T Batsford Limited
4 Fitzhardinge Street, London W1 and
Charles T Branford Company
28 Union Street, Newton Centre,
Boston, Massachusetts

Contents

Children's patterns

Soft furnishing

Introduction

Crochet is fashionable as never before. In Rome, Paris, London and New York, fashion designers have realised that the stitches of crochet, both simple and elaborate, can be used most effectively to form the fabric of elegant blouses and sportswear. Interior designers, too, appreciate how the patterns can be adapted to give a distinctive touch to the home for such things as cushion covers and bedspreads which have been developed from the traditional stitches.

Here is included a varied collection of designs and patterns both personal and practical. Even the beginner will find that the clear, easy to follow instructions and diagrams show all the stitches that are needed.

Instructions

Hand positions

Right handed people work from right to left.
Left handed people work from left to right.
The directions for each stitch apply to both right and left handed people.
For left handed people only; place a pocket mirror to the left of each illustration and you will see the exact position in which you work reflected in the mirror.

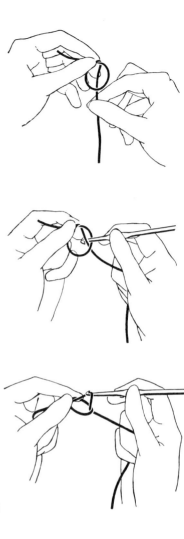

1

2

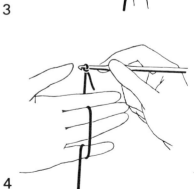

3

4

Step 1   Make a loop
1   Grasp yarn near end between thumb and forefinger.
2   Make a loop by lapping long yarn over short yarn.
3   Hold loop in place between thumb and forefinger (figure 1).

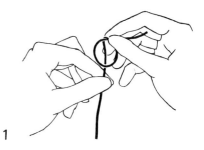

1

Step 2
1   Take hold of broad bar of hook as you would a pencil. Bring middle finger forward to rest near tip of hook.
2   Insert hook through loop and under long yarn. Catch long end of yarn (figure 2). Draw loop through.
3   Do not remove hook from yarn.

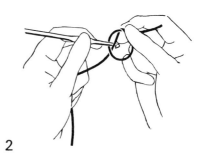

2

Step 3
1   Pull short end and ball yarn in opposite directions to bring loop close around the end of the hook, but not too tight (figure 3).

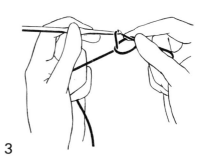

3

Step 4
1   Loop yarn round little finger, across palm and behind forefinger (figure 4).

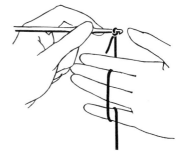

4

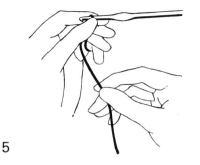

Step 5
1   Grasp hook and loop between thumb and forefinger.
2   Gently pull ball yarn so that it lies around the fingers firmly but not tightly (figure 5).
3   Catch knot of loop between thumb and forefinger.

5

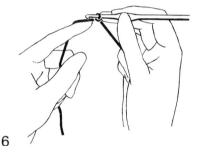

Step 6   Chain stitch
1   Adjust fingers as in figure 6. The middle finger is bent to regulate the tension; the ring and little fingers control the yarn. The motion of the hook in one hand and the yarn in the other hand should be free and even. Ease comes with practice.

6

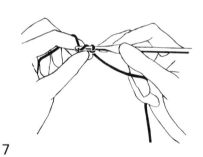

Step 7
1   Pass your hook under yarn and catch yarn with hook. This is called 'yarn over' (figure 7).
2   Draw yarn through loop on hook. This makes one chain (ch).

7

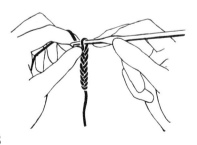

Step 8
1   Repeat step 7 until you have as many chain stitches (ch sts) as you need—1 loop always remains on the hook (figure 8).
2   Always keep thumb and forefinger near stitch on which you are working.
3   Practice making chain stitches until they are even in size.

8

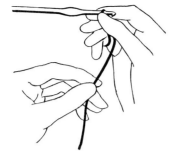

5

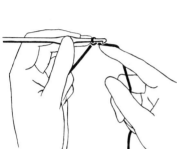

6

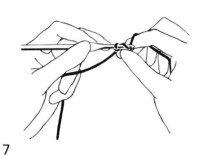

7

8

Slip stitch

8a

Insert hook from the front under the top threads of stitch to left of hook, catch yarn with hook and draw through stitch and loop on hook (figure 8a).

Abbreviations

B st	bead stitch
blks and sps	blocks and spaces
C	first contrasting colour
ch	chain
cl(s)	cluster(s)
Cr 2Tr	cross 2 treble
dec	decrease
dc	double crochet
dbl tr	double treble
hlf tr	half treble
hlf star	half star
inc	increase
lp(s)	loop(s)
M	main colour
p	picot
pc st(s)	popcorn stitch(es)
quad tr	quadruple treble
quin tr	quintuple treble
SC	second contrasting colour
sp(s)	space(s)
ss	slip stitch
st(s)	stitch(es)
st st	stocking stitch
TC	third contrasting colour
tr	treble
trip tr	triple treble

★ Asterisk

Repeat instructions following the asterisk as many more times as specified in addition to the original. For example ★ 1 dc into next cluster, 1 dc into next loop, 2 ch, 1 tr into next dc, 2 ch, 1 dc into next loop; repeat from ★ 9 times more, means that there are 10 patterns in all.
Repeat instructions in parenthesis as many times as specified.
For example, '(3 ch, 1 dc into next sp) 5 times', means to make all that is in parenthesis 5 times in all.

Synthetic yarns

The synthetic yarns of today possess many of the good properties of wool as well as outstanding inherent advantages of their own.

The yarns quoted in this book are of Coats *Carefree Bri-Nylon* and Coats *Cadenza Courtelle*. These yarns share many assets. Their range of colours, from clear pastels to rich dark tones, are completely fast and retain their brilliance throughout repeated laundering; even white remains pristine untainted by yellowing.

They are soft and pleasant to handle yet will stand any amount of hard wear and frequent washing: What could be better for sportswear, babywear and children's clothes? These yarns are easy to crochet and ideal for raised designs and fancy stitches; they refuse to become matted in washing and patterns remain clear and firm. Storage is no problem and garments can be packed away without fear of attack by moths or damage from damp.

Always purchase sufficient yarn of the same dye lot to complete the article.

Sizes

Figures in parenthesis refer to larger sizes. Where only one figure is given this refers to all sizes.

Tension

Tension in crochet is a very important feature particularly when garment sizing is involved. The tension quoted in the instructions must be achieved. A tension variation will make the finished article several inches larger or smaller than it should be. Before you crochet any design check your tension by working a section of the pattern and/or a motif and check the result with the tension stated in the instructions. If your tension is loose use a size finer hook; if tight use a size larger hook.

Making up garments

No matter how well you have crocheted the sections, the finished garment will look home made unless you take great care in the making up. Although it is a temptation to sew up the sections as soon as they are finished, time spent on preparation pays dividends in a more prefessional finish.

Lay an ironing sheet or a piece of white cotton over a blanket padding on a flat surface (a table or a carpet in a little used room). On this place each garment section wrong side up. Pat each piece into shape, and pin down round the edge with rustless pins. Cover the crochet with a clean damp sheet, and leave to dry naturally. Use a round pointed, large-eyed making up needle and the original yarn for sewing. If the yarn is too thick use a matching 3 ply or split the thick yarn and use a few strands. Pin all seams, matching the rows perfectly and oversew.

Helpful hints

As most garment instructions give more than one set of measurements it is advisable to read through the pattern before beginning to crochet. Find where your own bust size is in the bracket and underline that set of figures throughout the pattern.

Join a new ball of yarn at the beginning of a row. The odd length can be used for sewing up.

Remember to work exactly the same number of rows in pieces that are to be joined such as back and front; and if any alterations have been made to length or width take a note of them.

Washing instructions for Coats *Carefree Bri-Nylon* **and Coats** *Cadenza Courtelle*

Use warm suds (40°C, 104°F) for *Courtelle*, hand hot suds (48°C, 118°F) for *Bri-Nylon* and slightly hotter suds for white nylon.

Machine washing It is recommended that you follow the washing machine manufacturer's instructions for *Courtelle* and *Bri-Nylon*.

Hand washing Squeeze gently in suds (temperature according to the recommendation above). After washing, rinse thoroughly—at least twice—in warm water. (Give *Courtelle* an extra rinse in cold water.)

Remove excess moisture before putting to dry, either by rolling in a thick towel, or by wrapping in a towel and placing in a spin dryer for *a few seconds only*.

Drying *Do not drip dry*. Always dry flat. *Do not iron*, just smooth out any wrinkles or creases. Where picots, loops or scallops occur, pull them into shape. Avoid strong sunlight and direct heat of any kind.

Rows of double crocket

Note In all crochet it is customary to pick up the 2 top loops (or threads) of each stitch as you work, unless otherwise specified.

Make a starting chain of 20 stitches for practice piece.

First row (1st row)

9

Step 1 Insert hook from the front under the 2 top threads of 2nd ch from hook (figure 9).

10

Step 2 Catch yarn with hook—this is known as 'yarn over' (figure 10).

11

Step 3 Draw yarn through chain. There are 2 loops on hook (figure 11).

12

Step 4 Yarn over (figure 12) and draw through 2 loops—1 loop remains on hook.

13

Step 5 You have now completed 1 double crochet (dc) (figure 13).

Step 6 For next double crochet (dc) insert hook under 2 top threads of next ch and repeat Steps 2 to 6.

Step 7 Repeat Step 6 until you have made a double crochet (dc) in each ch.

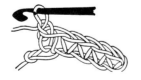

14

Step 8 At end of row of double crochet, work 1 ch (figure 14).
This 1 ch enables you to turn your work more easily but does not count as a stitch on next row.

14

15

Step 9 Turn your work so that the reverse side is facing you (figure 15).

Second row (2nd row)

Step 1 Insert hook from the front under the 2 top loops of first stitch (st)—the last dc made on previous row.

Step 2 Catch yarn with hook ('yarn over') and draw through st—2 loops remain on hook.

Step 3 Yarn over and draw through 2 loops—1 loop remains on hook.

Step 4 For next double crochet (dc), insert hook from the front under the 2 top loops of next st and repeat Steps 2 and 3.

Step 5 Repeat Step 4 until you have made a double crochet (dc) into each dc, 1 ch and turn.

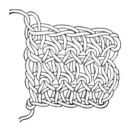

16

Step 6 Repeat Second row (2nd row) until you are familiar with this stitch. Fasten off (figure 16).

How to 'fasten off'

Step 1 Do not make a turning chain at end of last row.

Step 2 Cut yarn about 3 in. from work, bring loose end through the one remaining loop on hook and pull tightly (figure 16).

Rows of half treble crochet

Notice when working rows of half treble (hlf tr) that there is an extra loop on the wrong side directly below the 2 top loops of each hlf tr. Work only into the 2 top loops of each stitch. Make a starting chain of 20 stitches for practice piece.

First row (1st row)

17

Step 1 Pass hook under the yarn of left hand (this is called 'yarn over' figure 17).

Step 2 Insert hook from the front under the 2 top loops (or threads) of 3rd ch from hook.

18

Step 3 Yarn over hook and draw loop through ch (3 loops on hook), yarn over (figure 18).

19

Step 4 Draw through all loops on hook— 1 loop remains on hook (figure 19). A half treble (hlf tr) is now completed.

Step 5 For next half treble (hlf tr), yarn over, insert hook from front under the 2 top threads of next ch.

Step 6 Repeat Steps 3 to 5 until you have made a half treble (hlf tr) in each ch.

20

Step 7 At end of row, 2 ch (figure 20) and turn.

The turning 2 ch does not count as a stitch on the following rows.

Second row (2nd row)

Step 1 Yarn over hook, insert hook from front under the 2 top loops of first stitch (st)—the last hlf tr on previous row.

Step 2 Yarn over hook and draw through stitch—there are 3 loops on hook, thread over and draw through all loops on hook.

Step 3 For next half treble (hlf tr), yarn over hook, insert hook from the front under the 2 top loops of next stitch (st) and repeat Step 2.

Step 4 Repeat Step 3 until you have made a half treble (hlf tr) in each hlf tr, 2 ch and turn.

Step 5 Repeat Second row (2nd row) until you are familiar with this stitch. Fasten off at end of last row (figure 16).

Rows of treble crochet

Make a starting chain of 20 stitches for practice piece.

21

Step 1 Yarn over, insert hook from the front under the 2 top threads of 4th ch from hook (figure 21).

15

22

Step 2 Yarn over and draw through stitch (st). There are now 3 loops on hook (figure 22).

23

Step 3 Yarn over and draw through 2 loops —2 loops remain on hook (figure 23).

24

Step 4 Yarn over again and draw through the 2 remaining loops—1 loop remains on hook. One treble crochet (tr) is now completed (figure 24).

Step 5 For next treble crochet (tr), yarn over, insert hook from the front under the 2 top loops of next stitch (st) and repeat Steps 2 to 5 until you have made a treble crochet (tr) in each st.

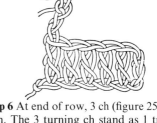

25

Step 6 At end of row, 3 ch (figure 25) and turn. The 3 turning ch stand as 1 tr and count as the first st in the following row.

Second row (2nd row)

Step 1 Yarn over, insert hook from the front under the 2 top loops of the 5th stitch from the hook (2nd stitch on previous row).

Step 2 Repeat Steps 2 to 7 of first row. Repeat the second row until you are familiar with this stitch. Fasten off.

How to 'turn your work'

In rows of crochet a certain number of chain stitches are added at the end of each row to bring the work into position for the next row. Then the work is turned so that the reverse side is facing the worker. The number of turning chain depends upon the stitch with which you intend to begin the next row.

Turning chain

dc — 1 ch
hlf tr — 2 ch
tr — 3 ch
dbl tr — 4 ch
trip tr — 5 ch
quad tr — 6 ch
quin tr — 7 ch

The above list gives the number of turning ch for each type of stitch which would be used when the following row is to be commenced with the same stitch. When applied to any of the stitches bracketed, the turning ch also stands as the first stitch of the next row.

16

Rounds of double crochet

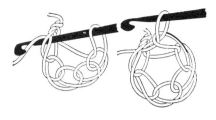

26   27

Step 1 Make a chain (ch) of 6 stitches (sts). Join with a slip stitch (ss) into 1st ch to form a ring (figures 26 and 27).

28

Step 2 1st row Make 8 double crochet (dc) into ring (figure 28). Place a safety pin in the last dc of 1st row to mark end of row. Move the safety pin to the last dc of the following rows.

29

Step 3 2nd row 2 double crochet (dc) into each dc of previous row—an increase made in each dc. There are 16 dc on row (figure 29).

Step 4 3rd row * 2 double crochet (dc) into next dc—an increase made in last dc (figure 29), 1 dc into next dc; repeat from * all round (24 dc on row).

Continue working in rows of double crochet as required, working increases wherever necessary in order to keep work flat and ending last row with 1 ss into each of next 2 dc. Fasten off.

Double treble

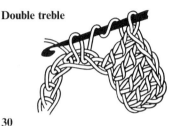

30

Pass hook under the yarn of left hand twice, insert hook into stitch to left of hook, yarn over hook and draw through stitch (4 loops on hook) (figure 30). Yarn over hook and draw through 2 loops on hook, yarn over hook and draw through other two loops on hook, yarn over and draw through remaining 2 loops (1 loop remains on hook).

Triple treble

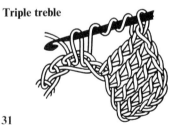

31

Pass hook under the yarn of left hand 3 times, insert hook into stitch to left of hook, yarn over hook and draw through stitch (5 loops on hook) (figure 31). Yarn over hook and draw through 2 loops on hook, (yarn over hook and draw through other 2 loops on hook) 3 times, 1 loop remains on hook.

17

Quadruple treble

Pass hook under the yarn of left hand 4 times and complete in same manner as trip tr until only 1 loop remains.

Quintuple treble

Pass hook under the yarn of left hand 5 times and complete in same manner as trip tr until only 1 loop remains.

Picot

32

Make a ch of 3, 4 or 5 sts according to length of picot (p) desired, join ch to form a ring working 1 dc into foundation or first ch (figure 32).

Clusters

Clusters may be worked in the following ways:

33

a A cluster worked over a given number of sts. Leaving the last loop of each on hook, work 1 dbl tr into each of next 4 sts, yarn over hook and draw through all loops on hook (a 4 dbl tr cluster made) (figure 33).

34

b A cluster worked into one stitch. Leaving the last loop of each stitch on hook, work 3 or more stitches into same stitch on previous row, yarn over and draw through all loops on hook (figure 34).

35

c A cluster worked into loop or space. Leaving the last loop of each stitch on hook, work 3 or more stitches into space or loop on previous row, yarn over and draw through all loops on hook (figure 35).

Filet crochet

The following four stitches are used mostly in Filet Crochet and are referred to as spaces, blocks, lacets and bars.

Space

36

Spaces are made with 2 ch, miss 2 stitches, 1 tr into next stitch (figure 36).

18

Blocks and spaces

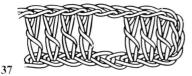

37

Work 1 tr into each of next 4 stitches, 2 ch, miss 2 stitches, 1 tr into next stitch, 1 tr into each of next 3 stitches (figure 37).

Bar and lacet

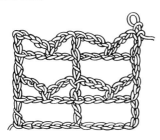

38

a ˜A bar consists of 5 ch, miss 5 stitches or a lacet, 1 tr into next stitch.
b A lacet consists of 3 ch, miss 2 stitches, 1 dc into next stitch, 3 ch, miss 2 stitches, 1 tr into next stitch (figure 38).

These are the correct numbers of Disc hooks to use with Coats Synthetic yarns

Yarns	Milward Disc crochet hooks
Carefree Bri-Nylon 3 ply	3·50 (no. 9)
Carefree Bri-Nylon 4 ply	4·00 (no. 8)
Cadenza Courtelle 4 ply	3·50 (no. 9)
Cadenza Courtelle Double Knitting	4·50 (no. 7)
Carefree Bri-Nylon Double Knitting	5·00 (no. 6)
Carefree Bri-Nylon Baby Quick Knit	5·00 (no. 6)
Coats *Baby Orlon*	3·50 (no. 9)

Metric conversion table

Ounce	Gram equivalent	20 gram ball	25 gram ball	50 gram ball
1	28·35	2	2	1
2	56·70	3	3	2
3	85·05	5	4	2
4	113·40	6	5	3
5	141·75	8	6	3
6	170·10	9	7	4
7	198·45	10	8	4
8	226·80	12	9	5
9	255·15	13	11	6
10	283·50	15	12	6
11	311·84	16	13	7
12	340·19	17	14	7
13	368·54	19	15	8
14	396·89	20	16	8
15	425·24	22	17	9
16	453·59	23	19	10
17	481·94	25	20	10
18	510·29	26	21	11
19	538·64	27	22	11
20	566·99	29	23	12
21	595·34	30	24	12
22	623·69	32	25	13
23	652·04	33	27	14
24	680·39	34	28	14
25	708·74	36	29	15

Showing gram equivalent to ounce of yarn

Ounce	Gram equivalent	20 gram ball	25 gram ball	50 gram ball
26	737·09	37	30	15
27	765·44	39	31	16
28	793·79	40	32	16
29	822·14	42	33	17
30	850·49	43	34	17
31	878·83	44	36	18
32	907·18	46	37	19
33	935·53	47	38	19
34	963·88	49	39	20
35	992·23	50	40	20
36	1020·58	51	41	21
37	1048·93	53	42	21
38	1077·28	54	44	22
39	1105·63	56	45	23
40	1133·98	57	46	23
41	1162·33	59	47	24
42	1190·68	60	48	24
43	1219·03	61	49	25
44	1247·38	63	50	25
45	1275·73	64	51	26
46	1304·08	66	53	27
47	1332·43	67	54	27
48	1360·78	68	55	28
49	1389·13	70	56	29
50	1417·48	71	57	30

Crochet hook size comparison chart

As from 1 July 1969, European Crochet hook manufacturers will be changing over to the New International Standard Range of crochet hooks. This chart shows both present and new ranges. The new range is illustrated in actual size, with the new size numbers alongside. There will be a change-over period of three to four years, at the end of which the old sizes will be withdrawn. Where the New International Standard Range has at present equivalents in steel and Disc (aluminium) crochet hooks, the steel hooks will be phased out. From this chart it will be easy to make comparisons between the old sizes as well as the new sizes which will be referred to in patterns in future.

By reference to the comparison chart it will be seen that the new range provides an adequate number of sizes to work all old patterns and to obtain the 'tension' required.

Milward new range of steel and aluminium crochet hooks. These hooks are shown in actual size with Present as well as New International numbering.	New Range International	Present Range Steel	Present Range Disc (aluminium)
		8	
		7	
		6½	
0.60 Milward 6	0.6	6	
		5½	
0.75 Milward 5	0.75	5	
		4½	
1.00 Milward 4	1	4	
		3½	
1.25 Milward 3	1.25	3	
1.50 Milward 2½	1.5	2½	
1.75 Milward 2	1.75	2	
		1½	
2.00 Milward 14	2	1	14
		1/0	
2.50 Milward 12	2.5	2/0	12
3.00 Milward 11	3	3/0	11
3.50 Milward 9	3.5		9
4.00 Milward 8	4		8
4.50 Milward 7	4.5		7
5.00 Milward 6	5		6
5.50 Milward 5	5.5		5
6.00 Milward 4	6		4
7.00 Milward 2	7		2

Jumper

Materials

8 (9, 10) oz Coats *Cadenza Courtelle* 4 ply Milward Disc (aluminium) crochet hook 3·50 (no. 9).

Measurements

To fit 34 to 36 (39 to 41) in. [86 to 92 (99 to 101) cm] bust
Length to top of shoulder (including edging) 23 (24) in. [58 (61) cm]
Sleeve seam (including edging) 3½ in. [89 mm]

Tension check

Before you crochet this design check your tension by working a 4½ in. [114 mm] square in the stitch pattern (33 ch and 16 rows). If your tension is loose use a size finer hook; if tight use a larger hook.

Back

Make 10 ch and leave aside for sleeve shaping.
Commence with 125 (151) ch to measure approximately 18 (22) in. [45 (56) cm].

1st row 1 hlf tr into 8th ch from hook, ★ miss 2 ch, 2 tr into each of next 5 ch, miss 2 ch, 1 hlf tr into next ch, 3 ch, miss 2 ch, 1 hlf tr into next ch; repeat from ★ ending with 5 ch, turn.

2nd row 1 dc into 3rd ch from hook, 1 hlf tr into first sp (a starting picot loop made), ★ 3 ch, miss 3 tr, 1 hlf tr into each of next 4 tr, 3 ch, 1 hlf tr into next lp, 3 ch, 1 dc into 3rd ch from hook (picot made), 1 hlf tr into same lp (a p lp made); repeat from ★ working last hlf tr into 5th of turning ch, 5 ch, turn.

3rd row miss p lp, ★ 1 hlf tr into next sp, 3 ch, 1 hlf tr between centre sts of next hlf tr group, 3 ch, 1 hlf tr into next sp, 4 ch; repeat from ★ ending last repeat with 3 ch, 1 hlf tr into 3rd of 5 ch, 3 ch, turn.

4th row 4 tr into first sp, ★ 1 hlf tr into next sp, 3 ch, 1 hlf tr into next sp, 10 tr into next sp; repeat from ★ omitting 6 tr at end of last repeat, 1 tr into 2nd of 5 ch, 2 ch, turn.

5th row miss first tr, 1 hlf tr into next tr, ★ 3 ch, a p lp into next sp, 3 ch, miss 3 tr, 1 hlf tr into each of next 4 tr; repeat from ★ omitting 2 hlf tr at end of last repeat and working last hlf tr into 3rd of 3 ch, 5 ch, turn.

6th row 1 hlf tr into first sp, ★ 4 ch, 1 hlf tr into next sp, 3 ch, 1 hlf tr between 2 centre sts of hlf tr group, 3 ch, 1 hlf tr into next sp; repeat from ★ omitting 3 ch and 1 hlf tr at end of last repeat and working last hlf tr into 2nd of 2 ch, 4 ch, turn.

7th row 1 hlf tr into first sp, 10 tr into next sp, ★ 1 hlf tr into next sp, 3 ch, 1 hlf tr into next sp, 10 tr into next sp; repeat from ★ ending with 1 hlf tr into last sp, 2 ch, 1 hlf tr into 2nd of 5 ch.

8th row As 2nd row working last hlf tr into

26

2nd of 4 ch, 5 ch, turn.

Last 6 rows form pattern.

Continue in pattern until work measures 14¼ in. [36 cm] or length required, ending with a 4th pattern row and turning with 11 ch at end of last row.

Sleeve shaping

1 hlf tr into 3rd ch from hook, 1 hlf tr into next ch, 3 ch, miss 2 ch, 1 hlf tr into next ch, 1 p, 1 hlf tr into next ch, 3 ch, miss 2 ch, 1 hlf tr into each of next 2 ch, 1 hlf tr into each of next 2 tr and continue in pattern to end of row, attach 10 ch already worked to top of turning ch on previous row and complete row thus: 1 hlf tr into each of next 2 ch, 3 ch, miss 2 ch, 1 hlf tr into next tr, 1 p, 1 hlf tr into next ch, 1 p, 1 hlf tr into next ch, 3 ch, miss 2 ch, 1 tr into each of next 2 ch, 5 ch, turn. ★★

Continue in pattern for 17 more rows (a 4th pattern row).

Neck shaping

1st row Work in pattern until 5th (6th) p lp has been worked, 3 ch, miss next 3 tr, 1 hlf tr into each of next 2 tr, 3 ch, turn.

2nd row 1 hlf tr into first sp, pattern to end.

3rd row Work in pattern until 5th (6th) group of 10 tr has been worked, 1 hlf tr into next sp, 3 ch, turn.

4th row Miss next 3 tr, 1 hlf tr into each of next 4 tr, pattern to end.

5th row Work in pattern until 1 hlf tr is worked between last 4 hlf tr group, 2 ch, 1 hlf tr into last sp, 3 ch, turn.

6th row Miss first sp, 1 hlf tr into next sp, 10 tr into next sp, pattern to end.

7th row Work in pattern ending with 2 ch, 1 hlf tr into last sp, 2 ch, turn.

8th row Miss first sp and 1 tr, 1 hlf tr between next 2 hlf tr, pattern to end.

9th row Work in pattern until 4th (5th) group of 10 tr has been worked, 1 hlf tr into next sp, 3 ch, turn.

10th row Miss next 3 tr, pattern to end.

1st size only

11th row Work in pattern to within last 4 hlf tr group. (10 sps.) Fasten off.

2nd size only

Repeat 5th to 8th row of neck shaping.

15th row Work in pattern until 4th group of 10 tr has been worked, 1 hlf tr into next sp, 3 ch, turn.

16th row Miss next 3 tr, pattern to end.

17th row Work in pattern to last sp. (12 sps.) Fasten off.

Miss centre sp and 4 tr, rejoin yarn to next tr, 2 ch, 1 hlf tr into next tr, pattern to end. Complete this side to correspond with other side.

Front

Work as for Back to ★★.
Continue in pattern for 5 more rows (a 4th pattern row).

Neck shaping

1st to 4th row As 1st to 4th row of back neck shaping.

5th row Work in pattern until 1 hlf tr is worked between last 4 hlf tr group, 3 ch, 1 hlf tr into last sp, 2 ch, turn.

6th row 1 hlf tr into first sp, 3 ch, 1 hlf tr into next sp, pattern to end.

7th row Work in pattern ending with 3 ch, 1 p lp into last 3 ch sp, 4 ch, turn.

8th row 1 hlf tr into first sp, pattern to end.

9th row Work in pattern until 4th (5th) group of 10 tr has been worked, 1 hlf tr into next sp, 3 ch, 1 hlf tr into next sp, 3 tr into

last sp, 3 ch, turn.

10th row 1 p lp into first sp, pattern to end.

11th row Work in pattern ending with 4 ch, 1 hlf tr into last sp, 3 ch, turn.

12th row 4 tr into first sp, pattern to end.

13th row Work in pattern until 4 (5) p lps have been worked, 3 ch, miss next 3 tr, 1 hlf tr into each of next 2 sts, 2 ch, turn.

14th row 1 hlf tr into first sp, pattern to end.

15th row Work in pattern ending with 1 hlf tr into last sp, 3 ch, turn.

16th row Miss first 3 tr, pattern to end.

17th row As 5th row.

18th row Miss first sp, 1 hlf tr into next sp, pattern to end.

19th row Work in pattern ending with a p lp into last sp, 3 ch, turn.

20th row 1 hlf tr into first sp, pattern to end.

21st row Work in pattern ending with 2 tr into last sp, 3 ch, turn.

22nd row 1 p lp into first sp, pattern to end.

1st size only

23rd row Work in pattern ending with 1 hlf tr into last sp. Fasten off.

2nd size only

Repeat 11th and 12th rows.

25th row Work in pattern until 4 p lps have been worked, 3 ch, miss next 3 tr, 1 hlf tr into each of next 2 sts, 2 ch, turn.

26th to 29th row As 14th to 17th row. Fasten off.

Miss centre sp and 4 tr, rejoin yarn to next tr and complete to correspond with other side.

To make up

Do not press.
Sew shoulder, side and sleeve seams.

Lower edging

1st row With right side facing attach yarn at side seam and work a row of dc evenly all round lower edge, 177 (195) dc approximately or a multiple of 3 dc, 1 ss into first dc.

2nd to 7th row 1 dc into same place as ss, 1 dc into each dc ending with 1 ss into first dc.

8th row 5 ch, 1 tr into same place as ss, * miss 2 ch, 1 tr 2 ch and 1 tr into next dc; repeat from * ending with 1 ss into 3rd of 5 ch.

9th row 1 dc 2 ch and 1 tr into same place as ss, * miss 2 ch and 1 tr, 1 dc 2 ch and 1 tr into next tr; repeat from * ending with 1 ss into first dc. Fasten off.

Neck edging

1st row With right side facing attach yarn at shoulder seam and work a row of dc evenly all round neck edge, 147 (195) dc approximately or a multiple of 3 dc, 1 ss into first dc.

2nd to 9th row As 2nd to 9th row of lower edging but missing 3 ch instead of 2 ch on each repeat of 8th row.

Sleeve edgings

1st row With right side facing attach yarn at underarm and work 65 (72) dc approximately or a multiple of 3 dc, 1 ss into first dc.

2nd to 9th row As 2nd to 9th row of lower edging.

Twin set

Materials

Jacket 10 (11, 12, 13) oz Coats *Cadenza Courtelle* Crepe knits as 4 ply
Blouse 6 (7, 7, 8) oz
Milward Disc (aluminium) crochet hook 3·50 (no. 9)
OR
Jacket 11 (12, 13, 14) oz Coats *Carefree Bri-Nylon* 4 ply
Blouse 7 (8, 8, 9) oz
Milward Disc (aluminium) crochet hook 4·00 (no. 8)

Measurements

Jacket To fit 34 (36, 38, 40) in. [86 (92, 96, 100) cm] bust
Length at centre back 21 (22, 23¼, 24¼) in. [52·5 (55, 59, 62) cm]
Sleeve seam 13 (13, 13¾, 13¾) in. [33 (33, 35, 35) cm]
Blouse To fit 34 (36, 38, 40) in. [86 (92, 96, 100) cm] bust
Length from shoulder 19½ (20½, 21½, 22½) in. [50 (52, 54, 57) cm]

Tension check

Before you crochet these designs check the tension by working an approximately 3 in. [76 mm] square in the stitch pattern (23 ch and 9 rows) using the size of hook stated. If your tension is loose use a size finer hook; if tight, use a size larger hook.

Tension

2 puff sts and 2 sps to 1 in. [25 mm].
First 3 rows to 1 in. [25 mm] approximately.

Jacket

Note   Back and fronts are worked as one to within armhole shaping.
Using 3·50 (no. 9) hook for *Cadenza*, 4·00 (no. 8) hook for *Carefree* commence with 221 (233, 245, 257) ch.

1st row 1 dc into 2nd ch from hook, * 3 ch, miss 2 ch, 1 dc into next ch; repeat from * to end, 3 ch, turn.

2nd row (right side) Yarn over hook, insert hook into centre ch of next lp and draw lp up ⅜ in. [10 mm] (yarn over hook insert hook into same ch and draw lp up as before) twice, yarn over and draw through all lps on hook—a puff st made, * 2 ch, a puff st into centre ch of next lp; repeat from * ending with 1 tr into last dc, 1 ch, turn.

3rd row 1 dc into first tr, * 3 ch, 1 dc into next sp; repeat from * ending with 3 ch, 1 dc into 3rd of 3 ch, 3 ch, turn.

2nd and 3rd rows form pattern.
Continue in pattern until work measures 13 (14, 14, 15) in. [33 (35, 35, 38) cm] ending with a 2nd pattern row.

Left front

Armhole shaping

1st row 1 dc into first tr, * 3 ch, 1 dc into next sp; repeat from * 15 (16, 17, 18) times more, 3 ch, turn. Work in pattern for 15 (15, 19, 19) rows more, omitting turning ch at end of last row.

Neck shaping

1st row 1 ss into each of first 11 (11, 14, 14) sts, 1 dc into next sp, work in pattern to end.

2nd row Work in pattern to within last 2 lps, 2 ch, a puff st into centre ch of next lp, 1 tr into centre ch of next lp, turn.

3rd row 1 ss into each of first 2 sts, 1 dc into next sp, work in pattern to end.

4th row Work in pattern ending with a puff st into centre ch of last lp, 1 tr into next dc, 1 ch, turn.

Shoulder shaping

1st row Work in pattern to within last 3 sps, turn.

2nd row 1 ss into each of first 7 sts, 2 ch, a puff st into centre ch of next lp, work in pattern to end omitting turning ch. Fasten off.

Back

Armhole shaping

1st row With wrong side facing miss next 4 puff sts, attach yarn to next sp, 1 dc into same place as join, * 3 ch, 1 dc into next sp;

repeat from * 32 (34, 36, 38) times more, 3 ch, turn.

Work in pattern for 19 (19, 23, 23) rows more omitting turning ch at end of last row.

Shoulder shaping

1st row 1 ss into each of first 11 sts, 1 dc into next sp, work in pattern to within last 4 sps, 3 ch, 1 dc into next sp, turn.

2nd row 1 ss into each of first 7 sts, 2 ch, a puff st into centre ch of next lp, work in pattern to within last 3 lps, 2 ch, a puff st into centre ch of next lp, 1 hlf tr into centre ch of next lp. Fasten off.

Right front

Armhole shaping

1st row With wrong side facing miss next 4 puff sts, attach yarn to next sp, 1 dc into same sp, 3 ch, work in pattern to end.

Work in pattern for 15 (15, 19, 19) rows more.

Neck shaping

1st row Work in pattern to within last 4 (4, 5, 5) sps, 3 ch, 1 dc into next sp, turn.

2nd row 1 ss into each of first 3 sts, 3 ch, a puff st into centre ch of next lp, work in pattern to end.

3rd row Work in pattern to within last sp, 3 ch, 1 dc into next sp, 3 ch, turn.

4th row Work in pattern omitting turning ch.

Shoulder shaping

1st row 1 ss into each of first 11 sts, 1 dc into next sp, work in pattern to end.

2nd row Work in pattern to within last 3 lps, 2 ch, a puff st into centre ch of next lp, 1 hlf tr into centre ch of next lp. Fasten off.

Sew shoulder seams.

Right sleeve

1st row Using 3·50 (no. 9) hook for *Cadenza*, 4·00 (no. 8) hook for *Carefree* and with right side facing attach yarn to first row end of Back armhole shaping, draw lp on hook up ⅜ in. [10 mm] (yarn over hook, insert hook into same place as join and draw lp up as before) twice, yarn over and draw through all lps on hook—a starting puff st made, remove lp from hook, insert hook into next puff st at underarm and draw dropped lp through—a joining ss made, (2 ch, a puff st over next row end) twice, (2 ch, miss next row end, a puff st over next row end) 7 (7, 9, 9) times, (2 ch, a puff st over next row end) twice, 2 ch, a puff st into shoulder seam, 2 ch, miss next row end, (a puff st over next row end, 2 ch) 3 times, (miss next row end, a puff st over next row end, 2 ch) 7 (7, 9, 9) times, a puff st over next row end, 2 ch, a puff st over next row end, 1 ss into next puff st at underarm, 1 ss into next sp, turn.

2nd row * 3 ch, 1 dc into next sp; repeat from * ending with 3 ch, 1 ss into next sp at underarm, turn.

3rd row 1 ss into each of first 2 ch, a starting puff st into same place as last ss, a joining ss into next puff st at underarm, * 2 ch, a puff st into centre ch of next lp; repeat from * ending with 1 ss into next puff st at underarm, 1 ss into next sp, 1 ch, turn.

4th row 1 dc into same place as last ss, * 3 ch, 1 dc into next sp; repeat from * ending with 3 ch, 1 ss into first dc, turn.

5th row 1 ss into each of first 2 ch, a starting puff st into same place as last ss, * 2 ch, a puff st into centre ch of next lp; repeat from * ending with 2 ch, 1 ss into starting puff st, turn.

6th row 1 ss into next sp, 1 dc into same sp, * 3 ch, 1 dc into next sp; repeat from * ending with 3 ch, 1 ss into first dc, turn.

Repeat last 2 rows 13 (13, 14, 14) times more, then 5th row again, do not turn or fasten off at end of last row.

32

Edging

1st row 2 dc into each sp, 1 ss into first dc.

2nd row 1 dc into same place as ss, 1 dc into each dc, 1 ss into first dc.

Repeat last row 4 times more. Fasten off.

Left sleeve

Using 3·50 (no. 9) hook for *Cadenza*, 4·00 (no. 8) hook for *Carefree* and with right side facing attach yarn to first row end of Front armhole shaping and complete to correspond with Right sleeve.

Outer edging

1st row Using 3·50 (no. 9) hook for *Cadenza*, 4·00 (no. 8) hook for *Carefree* and with right side of Left front facing attach yarn to first sp on lower edge after corner, work a row of dc evenly all round working 3 dc into each corner st and ending with 1 ss into into first dc.

2nd row 1 dc into same place as ss, 1 dc into each dc working 3 dc into centre dc at each corner, 1 ss into first dc.

Repeat last row 4 times more. Fasten off.

Blouse

Note Back and front are worked as one to within armhole shaping.
Using 3·50 (no. 9) hook for *Cadenza*, 4·00 (no. 8) hook for *Carefree* commence with 216 (228, 240, 252) ch, being careful not to twist, join with a ss to form a ring.

1st row 1 dc into same place as ss, * 3 ch, miss 2 ch, 1 dc into next ch; repeat from * ending with 3 ch, 1 ss into first dc, turn.

2nd row 1 ss into each of first 2 ch, a starting puff st into same place as last ss, * 2 ch, a puff st into centre ch on next lp; repeat from * ending with 2 ch, 1 ss into starting puff st, turn.

3rd row 1 ss into next sp, 1 dc into same sp, ★ 3 ch, 1 dc into next sp; repeat from ★ ending with 3 ch, 1 ss into first dc, turn.

Repeat last 2 rows until work measures 13 (14, 14, 15) in. [33 (35, 35, 38) cm] ending with a 2nd row.

Back

Armhole shaping

1st row 1 ss into each of next 3 sts, 1 dc into next sp, ★ 3 ch, 1 dc into next sp; repeat from ★ 31 (33, 35, 37) times more, turn.

2nd row 1 ss into each of first 7 sts, 3 ch, a puff st into centre ch of next lp, work in pattern to within last 3 lps, 2 ch, a puff st into centre ch of next lp, 1 tr into centre ch of next lp, 1 ch, turn.

Work in pattern for 10 rows more.

Neck shaping

1st row 1 dc into first tr, ★ 3 ch, 1 dc into next sp; repeat from ★ 8 (9, 9, 10) times more, turn.

2nd row 1 ss into each of first 3 sts, 3 ch, a puff st into centre ch of next lp, work in pattern to end.

3rd row Work in pattern to within last sp, 3 ch, 1 dc into next sp, turn.

Repeat last 2 rows once more, turning with 3 ch at end of last row.

Continue in pattern until armhole measures 6 (6, 7, 7) in. [152 (152, 175, 175) mm] ending with a 2nd pattern row and omitting turning ch at end of last row. Fasten off.
With wrong side facing miss 10 (10, 12, 12) puff sts at centre, attach yarn to next sp and complete to correspond with first side.

Front

Armhole shaping

1st row With wrong side facing miss next 4 puff sts, attach yarn to next sp, 1 dc into same sp, ★ 3 ch, 1 dc into next sp; repeat from ★ 31 (33, 35, 37) times more, turn. Complete to correspond with Back.

Sew shoulder seams.

Neck edging

1st row Using 3·50 (no. 9) hook for *Cadenza*, 4·00 (no. 8) hook for *Carefree* and with right side facing attach yarn to any shoulder seam, 1 dc into same place as join, work a row of dc evenly all round, 1 ss into first dc.

2nd row 1 dc into same place as ss, 1 dc into each dc, 1 ss into first dc.

3rd row As 2nd row. Fasten off.

Armhole edgings

As Neck edging.

Lower edging

1st row Using 3·50 (no. 9) hook for *Cadenza*, 4·00 (no. 8) hook for *Carefree* and with right side facing attach yarn to any sp on lower edge, work a row of dc evenly all round, 1 ss into first dc.

2nd and 3rd rows As 2nd and 3rd rows of Neck edging.

Sports sweater

Materials

12 (13, 14) oz Coats *Cadenza Courtelle*
Double Knitting main colour
10 (11, 12) oz contrasting colour
Milward Disc crochet hook 4·50 (no. 7).

Measurements

To fit 36 (38, 40) in. [86 (92, 96, 100) cm]
bust
Length from shoulder 23½ (24½, 25½) in.
[60 (62, 65) cm]
Sleeve seam 17 (18, 19) in. [43 (46, 48) cm]

Tension check

Before you crochet this design check the
tension by working an approximately 3 in.
[76 mm] square in the stitch pattern (16 ch
and 6 rows) using the size of hook stated. If
your tension is loose use a size finer hook;
if tight use a size larger hook.

Pattern tension

2 cls to 1 in. [25 mm] and 2 rows to 1 in.
[25 mm].

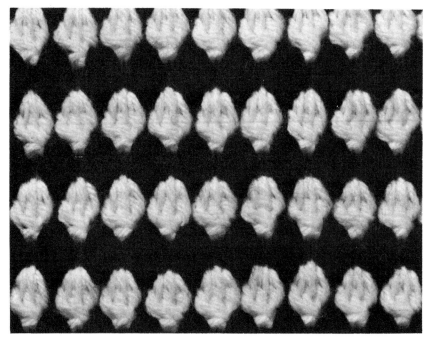

Note

The rows of this garment are always worked with right side facing and from right to left.

Back and front (alike)

Using M commence with 82 (86, 90) ch, to measure 19½ (20½, 21½) in. [50 (52, 54) cm].

1st row Leaving last lp of each on hook, work 3 tr into 4th ch from hook, yarn over and draw through all lps on hook—a 3 tr cl made, * 1 ch, miss 1 ch, a 3 tr cl into next ch; repeat from * ending with 1 ch, miss 1 ch, 1 tr into last ch. Fasten off.

2nd row Attach C to ch before first cl on previous row, 4 ch, * a 3 tr cl into next sp, 1 ch; repeat from * ending with a 3 tr cl into last sp, 1 tr into next tr. Fasten off.

3rd row Attach M to 3rd of 4 ch, 3 ch, a 3 tr cl into first sp, * 1 ch, a 3 tr cl into next sp; repeat from * ending with 1 ch, 1 tr into next tr. Fasten off.

2nd and 3rd rows form pattern.
Continue in pattern until work measures 15½ in. [39 cm], or length required, ending with a 3rd pattern row.

Armhole shaping

1st row Miss 2 cls, attach C to next cl, 3 ch, a 3 tr cl into next sp and work in pattern to within last 7 sts, 1 ch, 1 tr into next sp. Fasten off.

2nd row Attach M to 3rd of 3 ch, 4 ch and continue as 2nd pattern row to end.

3rd row Attach C to 3rd of 4 ch, 3 ch, a 3 tr cl into first sp and continue as 3rd pattern row to end.

Repeat last 2 rows 5 (6, 7) times more, then 2nd row once more.

36

Neck and shoulder shaping
First side

1st row Attach C to 3rd of 4 ch, 3 ch, a 3 tr cl into first sp, * 1 ch, a 3 tr cl into next sp; repeat from * 10 (11, 12) times more, 1 ch, 1 tr into next sp. Fasten off.

2nd row Attach M to 3rd of 3 ch, 4 ch, * a 3 tr cl into next sp, 1 ch; repeat from * 10 (11, 12) times more, 1 tr into last sp. Fasten off.

3rd row Miss first 4 cls, attach C to next cl, 4 ch, miss next sp, * a 3 tr cl into next sp, 1 ch; repeat from * 4 (5, 6) times more, 1 tr into next tr. Fasten off.

4th row Miss first cl, attach M into next sp, 4 ch, miss next sp, * a 3 tr cl into next sp, 1 ch; repeat from * 1 (2, 3) times more, a 3 tr cl into next sp, 1 tr into next tr. Fasten off.

Second side

1st row Miss 9 cls, attach C to next cl, 3 ch, * a 3 tr cl into next sp, 1 ch; repeat from * ending with 1 tr into next tr. Fasten off.

2nd row Attach M to first cl, 3 ch, * a 3 tr cl into next sp, 1 ch; repeat from * omitting 1 ch at end of last repeat, 1 tr into next tr. Fasten off.

3rd row Attach C to first cl, 3 ch, * a 3 tr cl into next sp, 1 ch; repeat from * 4 (5, 6) times more, miss next 2 sts, 1 tr into next cl. Fasten off.

4th row Attach M to 3rd of 3 ch, 4 ch, * a 3 tr cl into next sp, 1 ch; repeat from * 1 (2, 3) times more, a 3 tr cl into next sp, miss next 2 sts, 1 tr into next cl. Fasten off.

Sleeves

Using M commence with 32 ch.

1st row As 1st row of Back.

2nd row Attach C to ch before first cl on previous row, 4 ch, * a 3 tr cl into next sp, 1 ch; repeat from * ending with 1 tr into last tr. Fasten off. Inc made at end of row.

3rd row Attach M to 3rd of 4 ch, 4 ch, a 3 tr cl into first sp—inc made at beginning of row, * 1 ch, a 3 tr cl into next sp; repeat from * ending with 1 tr into last tr. Fasten off.

4th row Attach C to 3rd of 4 ch, 4 ch, a 3 tr cl into first sp—inc made at beginning of row, * 1 ch, a 3 tr cl into next sp; repeat from * ending with 1 ch, 1 tr into last tr. Fasten off.

5th row Attach M to 3rd of 4 ch, 3 ch, a 3 tr cl into first sp, * 1 ch, a 3 tr cl into next sp; repeat from * ending with 1 ch, 1 tr into last tr—inc made at end of row. Fasten off.

Repeat last 4 rows 4 (5, 6) times more. 24 (26, 28) cls.
Continue in pattern until work measures 17 (18, 19) in. [43 (46, 48) cm], or length required, ending with a 3rd pattern row.

Top shaping

1st row Miss 2 cls, attach C to next cl, 3 ch, * a 3 tr cl into next sp, 1 ch; repeat from * to within last 7 sts, miss next cl, 1 tr into next sp. Fasten off.

2nd row Attach M to first cl, 3 ch, * a 3 tr cl into next sp, 1 ch; repeat from * to within last 3 sts, 1 tr into next sp. Fasten off.

Keeping continuity of colours repeat last row 8 (9, 10) times more. Fasten off.

Collar

Using a back stitch seam, sew shoulder seams.

1st row With wrong side facing, attach M to first row end of Back at shoulder, 3 ch, a 2 tr cl into same place, 1 ch, into next row' end work a 3 tr cl 1 ch and a 3 tr cl, 1 ch, a 3

tr cl into next row end, 1 ch, into next row end work a 3 tr cl 1 ch and a 3 tr cl, (1 ch, a 3 tr cl into next sp) 9 times, (1 ch, into next row end work a 3 tr cl 1 ch and a 3 tr cl, 1 ch, a 3 tr cl into next row end) 4 times, (1 ch, a 3 tr cl into next sp) 9 times, (1 ch, a 3 tr cl into next row end, 1 ch, into next row end work a 3 tr cl 1 ch and a 3 tr cl) twice, 1 ch, 1 ss into first cl.

2nd and 3rd rows 1 ss into next sp, 3 ch, a 2 tr cl into same sp, * 1 ch, a 3 tr cl into next sp; repeat from * ending with 1 ch, 1 ss into first cl.

4th row As 2nd row, working a 3 tr cl 1 ch and a 3 tr cl into sp at each shoulder.

5th and 6th rows As 2nd row.

7th to 9th row As 4th row. Fasten off.

10th row Attach C to any sp, 3 ch and continue as 4th row.

11th row As 4th row. Fasten off.

To make up

Do not press.
Using a back stitch seam set in sleeves, sew side and sleeve seams.

Lower edging

1st row Using M attach yarn to base of cl at side seam, 1 dc into same place as join, * 1 dc into next sp, 1 dc into base of next cl; repeat from * ending with 1 dc into next sp, 1 ss into first dc.

2nd row 1 dc into each dc decreasing 8 sts evenly all round. Fasten off.

Jumper suit

Materials

14 (15, 16) oz Coats *Cadenza Courtelle* 4 ply
main colour
4 (5, 5) oz first contrasting colour
4 (5, 5) oz second contrasting colour
Milward Disc (aluminium) crochet hooks
3·50 (no. 9) and 3·00 (no. 11)
OR
16 (17, 18) oz Coats *Carefree Bri-Nylon*
4 ply main colour
5 (6, 6) oz first contrasting colour
5 (6, 6) oz second contrasting colour
Milward Disc (aluminium) crochet hooks
4·00 (no. 8) and 3·50 (no. 9)

5 in. [127 mm] 'LIGHTNING' Gold Pack
(Nylon) Zip
Length of elastic 1 in. [25 mm] wide to fit
waist.

Measurements

Jumper To fit 34 (36, 38) in. [86 (92, 96) cm]
bust
Length at centre back 22½ (23½, 23½) in. [57
(60, 60) cm]
Sleeve seam 12 (12, 13½) in. [30 (30, 34) cm]
Skirt To fit 36 (38, 40) in. [92 (96, 100) cm]
hip
Length 21 in. [53 cm] adjustable

38

Tension

Skirt 6 dc to 1 in. [25 mm] ⎫ Using smaller
    7 rows to 1 in. ⎬ size of hook.
    [25 mm] ⎭
Jumper 4 dbl tr and 1 dc to ⎫
    1 in. [25 mm] ⎪ Using larger
    2 rows to ¾ in. ⎬ size of hook.
    [19 mm] ⎭

Tension check

Before you crochet this design check the
tension by working an approximately 4½ in.
[114 mm] square in the jumper pattern (22
ch and 12 rows) using the larger size of
hook stated. If your tension is loose use a
size finer hook; if tight use a size larger
hook.

Skirt

Back and front

Using 3·00 (no. 11) hook for *Cadenza*, 3·50
(no. 9) hook for *Carefree* and M, commence with 95 (100, 105) ch.

1st row 1 dc into 2nd ch from hook, 1 dc
into each ch, 1 ch, turn.

2nd row 1 dc into each dc, 1 ch, turn.

Repeat last row 7 times more.

Next row 2 dc into first dc, 1 dc into each dc
to within last dc, 2 dc into last dc, 1 ch,
turn. (1 dc increased at beginning and end
of row.)

Repeat 2nd row 7 times more.
Repeat last 8 rows until there are 112 (117,
122) dc.
Repeat 2nd row until work measures 21 in.
[53 cm], or length required, omitting turning ch at end of last row. Fasten off.

Jumper

Back

Using 3·50 (no. 9) hook for *Cadenza*, 4·00 (no. 8) hook for *Carefree* and M, commence with 92 (97, 102) ch.

1st row 1 dc into 2nd ch from hook, * 4 ch, leaving the last lp of each on hook work 1 dbl tr into each of next 4 ch, yarn over and draw through all lps on hook—a 4 dbl tr cl made, 4 ch, 1 dc into next ch; repeat from * omitting 1 dc at end of last repeat, insert hook into next ch and draw yarn through, drop M, pick up C and draw through 2 remaining lps (always change colours in this manner), 4 ch, turn.

2nd row (right side) 2 dbl tr into first dc, * 1 dc into next cl, 4 dbl tr into next dc; repeat from * omitting 1 dbl tr at end of last repeat, 1 ch, turn.

3rd row 1 dc into first dbl tr, * 4 ch, a 4 dbl tr cl over next 4 dbl tr, 4 ch, 1 dc between last dbl tr and next dbl tr; repeat from * working last dc into 4th of 4 ch, changing to SC as before, 4 ch, turn.

4th row As 2nd row.

5th row As 3rd row, changing to M as before.

6th row As 2nd row.

7th row As 3rd row, changing to C as before.

2nd to 7th row forms colour pattern.
Keeping formation of colours, continue in pattern for 31 rows more, or length required, ending with a 2nd pattern row and omitting turning ch at end of last row.

Armhole shaping

1st row 1 ss into each of first 6 sts, 1 dc between last dbl tr and next dbl tr, 4 ch, work in pattern to within last 6 sts, 4 ch, 1 dc between last dbl tr and next dbl tr, turn.

2nd row Keeping formation of colours, miss first 5 sts, attach yarn to next cl, 1 dc into same place as join, work in pattern ending with 1 dc into last cl, turn.

3rd row 1 ss into each of first 3 sts, 1 dc between last dbl tr and next dbl tr, 4 ch, work in pattern to within last 3 sts, 1 dc between last dbl tr and next dbl tr, changing colours as before, 4 ch, turn.

Keeping formation of colours continue in pattern for 7 (9, 9) rows more.

Back opening 1st side

34 in. and 38 in. [86 cm and 96 cm] sizes only

1st row 1 dc into first dbl tr, * 4 ch, a 4 dbl tr cl over next 4 dbl tr, 4 ch, 1 dc between last dbl tr and next dbl tr; repeat from * 6 (7) times more, changing colours as before, 4 ch, turn.

Work in pattern for 7 rows more omitting turning ch at end of last row.

36 in. [91 cm] size only

1st row 1 dc into first dbl tr, * 4 ch, a 4 dbl tr cl over next 4 dbl tr, 4 ch, 1 dc between last dbl tr and next dbl tr; repeat from * 6 times more, 1 dc between last dbl tr and next dbl tr, 4 ch, a 2 dbl tr cl over next 2 dbl tr, changing colours as before, 1 ch, turn.

2nd row 1 dc into first cl, 4 dbl tr into next dc, work in pattern to end.

3rd row Work in pattern to within last 3 sts, 4 ch, a 3 dbl tr cl over next 3 sts, changing colours as before, 1 ch, turn.

Repeat last 2 rows twice more then 2nd row again, omitting turning ch at end of last row.

Shoulder shaping

34 in. and 38 in. [86 cm and 96 cm] sizes only

1st row 1 ss into each of first 8 sts, 1 dc into each of next 2 sts, 1 tr into next st, a 4 dbl tr cl over next 4 dbl tr, work in pattern to end.

2nd row Work in pattern to within last 3 sts. Fasten off.

36 in. [91 cm] size only

1st row 1 ss into each of first 8 sts, 1 dc into

each of next 2 sts, 1 tr into next st, a 4 dbl tr cl over next 4 dbl tr, work in pattern to within last 3 sts, a 3 dbl tr cl over next 3 sts, change colours, 1 ch, turn.

2nd row 1 dc into first cl, 4 dbl tr into next dc, work in pattern to within last 3 sts. Fasten off.

Back opening 2nd side

34 in. and 38 in. [86 cm and 96 cm] sizes only

1st row With wrong side facing, and keeping formation of colours, attach yarn to same place as last dc on 1st row of Back opening, 4 ch, a 4 dbl tr cl over next 4 dbl tr, work in pattern to end and complete to correspond with other side.

36 in. [91 cm] size only

1st row With wrong side facing, and keeping formation of colours, miss 1 dc at centre, attach yarn to next dbl tr, 4 ch, 1 dbl tr into next dbl tr, 1 dc between last dbl tr and next dbl tr, work in pattern to end and complete to correspond with other side.

Front

Work as Back until 3rd row of armhole shaping has been completed. Continue in pattern for 9 (11, 11) rows more.

Neck shaping 1st side

1st row 1 dc into first dbl tr, * 4 ch, a 4 dbl tr cl over next 4 dbl tr, 4 ch, 1 dc between last dbl tr and next dbl tr; repeat from * 4 (4, 5) times more, 4 ch, a 4 dbl tr cl over next 4 dbl tr, change colours, 1 ch, turn.

2nd row 4 dbl tr into first dc, work in pattern to end.

3rd row Work in pattern to within last 2 dbl tr, change colours, 1 ch, turn.

4th row As 2nd row.

5th row As 3rd row ending with 4 ch, turn.

6th row Work in pattern, omitting turning ch.

Shoulder shaping

7th row 1 ss into each of first 8 sts, 1 dc into each of next 2 sts, 1 tr into next st, work in pattern to end.

8th row Work in pattern to within last 3 sts. Fasten off.

Neck and shoulder shaping 2nd side

With wrong side facing miss 10 (15, 10) sts across front, keeping formation of colours, attach yarn to next st, 4 ch, a 3 dbl tr cl over next 3 dbl tr, and complete to correspond with other side.

Sleeves

Using 3·50 (no. 9) hook for *Cadenza*, 4·00 (no. 8) hook for *Carefree* and M, commence with 57 (62, 67) ch and work as Back for 26 (26, 32) rows, turning with 4 ch at end of last row.

1st inc row 1 dbl tr into first dbl tr, a 4 dbl tr cl over next 4 dbl tr, work in pattern to within last 6 sts, a 4 dbl tr cl over next 4 dbl tr, 2 dbl tr into 4th of 4 ch, change colours as before, 1 ch, turn.

2nd inc row 1 dc into first dbl tr, 3 dbl tr into next dbl tr, 1 dc into next cl, work in pattern to within last 2 sts, 3 dbl tr into next st, 1 dc into 4th of 4 ch, 4 ch, turn.

3rd inc row 1 dbl tr into first dbl tr, 4 ch, 1 dc between last dbl tr and next dbl tr, work in pattern to within last 2 sts, 1 dc between last dbl tr and next dbl tr, 4 ch, a 2 dbl tr cl over last 2 sts, change colours, 1 ch, turn.

4th inc row 1 dc into first cl, 4 dbl tr into next dc, work in pattern to within last 2 sts, 1 dc into 4th of 4 ch, 1 ch, turn.

5th inc row 1 dc into first dc, 4 ch, a 2 dbl tr cl over next 2 dbl tr, 4 ch, work in pattern to within last 3 sts, a 2 dbl tr cl over next 2 dbl tr, 4 ch, 1 dc into next dc, change colours, 4 ch, turn.

6th inc row Work in pattern omitting turning ch.

Top shaping

1st row 1 ss into each of first 7 sts, 4 ch, a 3 dbl tr cl over next 3 dbl tr, work in pattern to within last 11 sts, a 4 dbl tr cl over next 4 dbl tr, change colours, 1 ch, turn.

2nd row 1 dc into first cl, work in pattern omitting turning ch.

3rd row 1 ss into each of first 2 sts, 1 dc between next 2 dbl tr, work in pattern to within last 3 sts, 4 ch, 1 dc between same dbl tr and next dbl tr, change colours, 4 ch, turn.

4th row 1 dbl tr into first dc, 1 dc into next cl, work in pattern to within last dc, 2 dbl tr into last dc, 4 ch, turn.

5th row Miss first dbl tr, a 3 dbl tr cl over next 3 dbl tr, work in pattern to within last 5 sts, a 4 dbl tr cl over next 3 dbl tr and 4th of 4 ch, change colours, 1 ch, turn.

6th row 1 dc into first cl, work in pattern ending with 1 dc into last cl, turn.

7th row 1 ss into each of first 2 sts, 4 ch, 1 dbl tr into next dbl tr, a 4 dbl tr cl over next 4 dbl tr, work in pattern to within last 8 sts, a 4 dbl tr cl over next 4 sts, 1 dbl tr into each of next 2 dbl tr, change colours, 1 ch, turn.

8th row Miss first dbl tr, 1 dc into next dbl tr, 1 dc into next cl, work in pattern to within last 2 sts, 1 dc into next dbl tr, 4 ch, turn.

9th row Miss first st, a 3 dbl tr cl over next 3 sts, work in pattern to within last 4 sts, a 4 dbl tr cl over next 4 sts, change colours, 1 ch, turn.

10th to 12th row As 6th to 8th row, omitting turning ch at end of last row. Fasten off.

Neck edging

Using a flat seam sew side and sleeve seams.

1st row Using 3·50 (no. 9) hook for *Cadenza*, 4·00 (no. 8) hook for *Carefree*, M and with right side facing, attach yarn to back opening, 1 dc into same place as join, work

42

a row of dc evenly round neck edge, 1 ch, turn.

2nd row 1 dc into each dc, 1 ch, turn.

Repeat last row 7 times more omitting turning ch at end of last row. Fasten off.

Sleeve edging

1st row Using 3·50 (no. 9) hook for *Cadenza*, 4·00 (no. 8) hook for *Carefree*, M and with right side facing, attach yarn to sleeve seam, 1 dc into same place as join, work a row of dc evenly all round, 1 ss into first dc, 1 ch, turn.

2nd row 1 dc into each dc, 1 ss into first dc, 1 ch, turn.

Repeat 2nd row 3 times more omitting turning ch at end of last row. Fasten off.

Lower edging

1st row Using 3·50 (no. 9) hook for *Cadenza*, 4·00 (no. 8) hook for *Carefree*, M and with right side facing, attach yarn to any side seam, 1 dc into same place as join, work a row of dc evenly all round, 1 ss into first dc, 1 ch, turn.

Repeat 2nd row of sleeve edging twice more omitting turning ch at end of last row. Fasten off.

To make up

Do not press.

Skirt

Using a flat seam sew side seams. Join elastic to form a circle and using a herring bone casing attach to skirt on wrong side at waist.

Jumper

Sew zip in position. Using a flat seam set in sleeves. Press all seams lightly on the wrong side with a cool iron.

Blouse

Materials

5 (6, 6) oz Coats *Carefree Bri-Nylon* 3 ply
main colour
1 oz contrasting colour
Milward Disc (aluminium) crochet hooks
4·00 (no. 8), 3·50 (no. 9)
Two buttons

Measurements

To fit 32 (34, 36) in. [80 (86, 92) cm] bust
Length from shoulder 19½ (20½, 21½) in.
[50 (52, 54) cm] approximately

Tension

10 ch and 5 rows to 2 in. [50 mm].

Tension check

Before you crochet this design check your
tension by working an approximate 6 in.
[152 mm] square in the stitch pattern (34
ch and 15 rows). If your tension is loose
use a size finer hook; if tight use a size
larger hook.

Back

Using M and 4·00 (no. 8) hook commence
with 88 (94, 100) ch.

1st row 4 tr into 7th ch from hook—shell
made, * 1 ch, miss 2 ch, 1 tr into next ch, 1
ch, miss 2 ch, a shell into next ch; repeat
from * ending with 1 ch, miss 2 ch, 1 tr into
next ch, 4 ch, turn.

2nd row (right side) Miss first tr of next
shell, a shell between next 2 tr—shell made
over shell, * 1 ch, 1 tr into next tr, 1 ch, a
shell over next shell; repeat from * ending
with 1 ch, miss 1 ch, 1 tr into next ch, 3 ch,
turn.

3rd row 1 tr into first tr, 1 ch, miss 1 tr, 1 tr
between next 2 tr—1 tr made over shell, * 1
ch, a shell into next tr, 1 ch, 1 tr over next
shell; repeat from * ending with 1 ch, 2 tr
into 3rd of 4 ch, 3 ch, turn.

4th row 1 tr into first tr, 1 ch, miss 1 tr, * 1 tr
into next tr, 1 ch, a shell over next shell, 1
ch; repeat from * ending with 1 tr into next
tr, 1 ch, 2 tr into 3rd of 3 ch, 4 ch, turn.

5th row Miss first 2 tr, * a shell into next tr,
1 ch, 1 tr over next shell, 1 ch; repeat from
* omitting 1 tr and 1 ch at end of last repeat,
1 tr into 3rd of 3 ch, 4 ch, turn.

2nd to 5th row forms pattern.

Continue in pattern until work measures
14 in. [35 cm], or length required, ending
with a 3rd pattern row omitting turning
ch at end of last row.

Armhole shaping

1st row 1 ss into each of first 11 sts, 3 ch, a shell over next shell, work in pattern to within last 2 shells, a shell over next shell, 1 tr into next tr, 2 ch, turn.

2nd row 1 tr over next shell, a shell into next tr, work in pattern to within last shell, leaving the last lp of each on hook work 1 tr over next shell and 1 tr into 3rd of 3 ch, yarn over and draw through all lps on hook —a joint tr made, 3 ch, turn.

3rd row A shell over next shell, work in pattern to within last shell, a shell over next shell, 1 tr into next tr, 2 ch, turn.

Repeat last 2 rows once more turning with 3 ch at end of last row.

Work in pattern for 5 rows more.

Neck shaping

1st row 1 tr into first tr, 1 ch, miss 1 tr, 1 tr into next tr, 1 ch, a shell over next shell, 1 ch, 1 tr into next tr, 1 ch, 2 tr over next shell, 4 ch, turn.

Work in pattern for 4 (6, 8) rows more omitting turning ch at end of last row. Fasten off.

With right side facing miss 4 (5, 6) shells at centre, attach yarn between centre 2 tr on next shell, 3 ch, 1 tr into same place as join and complete to correspond with first side.

Front

Work as Back until 6th row of armhole shaping has been completed.

Neck shaping

Work as Back neck shaping.

With right side facing miss 4 (5, 6) shells at centre, attach yarn between centre 2 tr on next shell, 3 ch, 1 tr into same place as join and complete to correspond with first side.

To make up

Do not press. Sew side seams.

Neck and armhole edging

1st row Using M and 3·50 (no. 9) hook attach yarn to any underarm seam, 1 dc into same place as join, work a row of dc evenly all round, 1 ss into first dc. Drop M, pick up C.

2nd row 1 dc into same place as ss, 1 dc into each dc, 1 ss into first dc.

Repeat last row twice more. Fasten off.

Lower edging

1st row Using M and 3·50 (no. 9) hook attach yarn to any side seam, 1 dc into same place as join, work a row of dc evenly all round, 1 ss into first dc. Drop M, pick up C.

2nd row As 2nd row of Neck and armhole edging.

Repeat last row 3 times more. Fasten off.

To complete

Overlap back shoulder straps to front and sew buttons centrally in position.

Evening blouse

Materials

9 (10, 11) oz Coats *Cadenza Courtelle* Double Crepe
OR
7 (8, 9) oz Coats *Cadenza Courtelle* Double Knitting
Milward Disc crochet hook 4·50 (no. 7).

Measurements

To fit 34 (36, 38) in. [86 (92, 96) cm] bust
Length from shoulder 19 (20, 21½) in. [48 (51, 54) cm]

Tension check

Before you crochet this design check the tension by working a 3 in. [76 mm] square in the V stitch pattern (17 ch and 7 rows) using the size of hook stated. If your tension is loose use a size finer hook; if tight use a size larger hook.

Pattern tension

2 V sts to 1¼ in. [32 mm].
2 V sts and 1 shell to 2½ in. [64 mm].

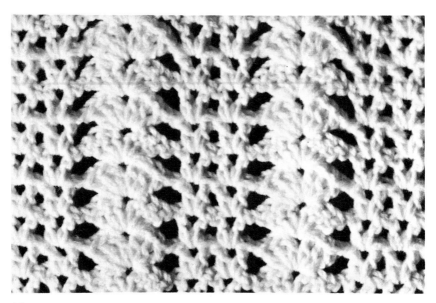

47

Back and front (both alike)

Commence with 81 (87, 93) ch.

1st row (right side) Into 6th ch from hook work 1 tr 1 ch and 1 tr—a V st made, (miss 2 ch, a V st into next ch) 6 (7, 8) times, * 1 ch, miss 2 ch, (3 tr into next ch, 1 ch) twice, (miss 2 ch, a V st into next ch) twice; repeat from * 3 times more, (miss 2 ch, a V st into next ch) 5 (6, 7) times more, 1 ch, miss 1 ch, 1 tr into next ch, 4 ch, turn.

2nd row A V st into sp of first V st—a V st made over a V st, (a V st over next V st) 6 (7, 8) times more, * 1 ch, miss next sp, into next sp work 3 tr 1 ch and 3 tr—a shell made, 1 ch, (a V st over next V st) twice; repeat from * 3 times more, (a V st over next V st) 5 (6, 7) times more, 1 ch, miss 1 ch, 1 tr into next ch, 4 ch, turn.

2nd row forms pattern.
Continue in pattern until work measures 12 in. [3 cm], or length required, omitting turning ch at end of last row.

Armhole shaping

1st row 1 ss into each of first 3 sts and into next sp, 3 ch, a V st over next V st, work in pattern to within last V st, 1 tr into next V st, turn.

2nd row Miss first tr, 1 ss into next tr and into next sp, 3 ch, a V st over next V st, work in pattern to within last V st, 1 tr into next V st, turn.

Repeat 2nd row 2 (3, 3) times more turning with 4 ch at end of last row.
Continue in pattern for 3 (4, 5) rows more.

Next row (A V st over next V st) 3 (3, 4) times, * 3 ch, 1 dc into centre of next shell, 3 ch, (a V st over next V st) twice; repeat from * 3 times more, (a V st over next V st) 1 (1, 2) times, 1 ch, 1 tr into 3rd of 4 ch, 4 ch, turn.

Neck shaping

1st row (A V st over next V st) 3 (3, 4) times, 1 ch, 1 tr into next dc, 4 ch, turn.

2nd row (A V st over next V st) 3 (3, 4) times, 1 ch, 1 tr into 3rd of 4 ch, 4 ch, turn.

Repeat 2nd row 5 (6, 7) times more omitting turning ch at end of last row.
Fasten off.
Miss 2 dc at centre, attach yarn to next dc, 4 ch and complete to correspond with first side.

To make up

Do not press.
Oversew shoulder and side seams.

Neck edging

1st row With right side facing attach yarn to any shoulder seam, 1 dc into same place as join, work a row of dc evenly all round having a multiple of 4 dc, 1 ss into first dc.

2nd row 1 dc into same place as ss, * miss next dc, 4 tr into next dc, miss next dc, 1 dc into next dc; repeat from * omitting 1 dc at end of last repeat, 1 ss into first dc. Fasten off.

Armhole edgings

With right side facing attach yarn to under-arm seam and work as Neck edging.

Lower edging

With right side facing attach yarn to any side seam and work as Neck edging.

Two colour slip over blouse

Materials

4 (5, 5) oz Coats *Carefree Bri-Nylon* 3 ply
in main colour
2 (2, 3) oz in contrasting colour
Milward Disc (aluminium) crochet hook
3·50 (no. 9).

Measurements

To fit 32 (34, 36) in. [80 (86, 92) cm] bust
Length from shoulder 21 in. [52·5 cm]

Tension

4 rows to 2 in. [50 mm].

Tension check

Before you crochet this design check your
tension by working an approximate 4 in.
[102 mm] square in the stitch pattern (28 ch
and 8 rows). If your tension is loose use a
size finer hook; if tight use a larger size
hook.

Back and front (both alike)

Using M, commence with 108 (118, 128) ch
(approximately 16 (17, 18) in. [40 (43, 46)
cm] long).

1st row Into 6th ch from hook work 1 dbl tr
3 ch and 1 dbl tr (V st made), * miss 4 ch, 5
dbl tr into next ch (shell made), miss 4 ch,
V st into next ch; repeat from * ending with
miss 1 ch, 1 dbl tr into next ch, 4 ch, turn.

2nd row V st into sp of first V st, * 1 dbl tr into each dbl tr of next shell, V st into sp of next V st; repeat from * ending with 1 dbl tr into top of turning ch, 4 ch, turn.

3rd row 4 dbl tr into sp of first V st, * V st into centre dbl tr of next shell, shell into sp of next V st; repeat from * working last dbl tr into 4th of 4 ch, 4 ch, turn.

4th row Miss first dbl tr, 1 dbl tr into each of next 4 dbl tr, * V st into sp of next V st, 1 dbl tr into each dbl tr of next shell; repeat from * working last dbl tr into 4th of 4 ch, 4 ch, turn.

5th row Miss first 2 dbl tr, V st into next dbl tr, * shell into sp of next V st, V st into centre dbl tr of next shell; repeat from * ending with 1 dbl tr into 4th of 4 ch, 4 ch, turn.

Last 4 rows form pattern.
Repeat pattern 6 times more, then 2nd to 4th row once more.

Neck shaping

1st row Miss first 2 dbl tr, V st into next dbl tr, shell into sp of V st, (V st into centre dbl tr of next shell, shell into sp of next V st) 1 (1, 2) times, 1 dbl tr into centre dbl tr of next shell, 4 ch, turn.

Work in pattern for 5 rows more. Fasten off.
Miss 5 (6, 5) shells, attach yarn to centre dbl tr of next shell, 4 ch, shell into next V st and complete to correspond with first side. Sew shoulder seams.

Side edging

1st row Using C, attach yarn to end of first row, 3 ch, 2 hlf tr into same row-end, * 1 ch, 2 hlf tr into next row-end; repeat from * across one side of back and front, 3 ch, turn.

2nd row 2 hlf tr into first 1 ch sp, * 1 ch, 2 hlf tr into next 1 ch sp; repeat from * ending with 1 ch, 2 hlf tr into last sp, 3 ch, turn.

Repeat 2nd row 6 times more omitting turning ch at end of last row. Fasten off.

Work across other side to correspond.
Leaving approximately $7\frac{1}{2}$ in. [19 cm] open on each side of shoulder seam for armhole, sew side seams.

Neck edging

1st row Using C, attach yarn to row-end before shoulder seam, 2 ch, 1 hlf tr into same row-end, * (1 ch, 2 hlf tr into next row-end) 6 times, (1 ch, 2 hlf tr into sp of next V st 1 ch, 2 hlf tr into centre dbl tr of next shell) 5 (6, 5) times, 1 ch, 2 hlf tr into sp of next V st, (1 ch, 2 hlf tr into next row-end) 6 times; repeat from * once more, omitting 2 hlf tr at end of repeat, 1 ss into first hlf tr.

2nd row Ss into first 1 ch sp, 2 ch, 1 hlf tr into same sp, * 1 ch, 2 hlf tr into next sp; repeat from * ending with 1 ch, 1 ss into 2nd of 2 ch.

Repeat last row 6 times more. Fasten off.

Lower edging

Using C, attach yarn to turning ch before side seam, 2 ch, 1 hlf tr into same turning ch, * (1 ch, 2 hlf tr over next turning ch) 4 times, 1 ch, 2 hlf tr over first sp on foundation ch, (1 ch, 2 hlf tr into same ch as next V st, 1 ch, 2 hlf tr into next sp, 1 ch, 2 hlf tr into same ch as next shell, 1 ch, 2 hlf tr into next sp) 10 (11, 12) times, 1 ch, 2 hlf tr into same ch as next V st, 1 ch, 2 hlf tr into next sp, (1 ch, 2 hlf tr into next turning ch) 4 times; repeat from * once more omitting 2 hlf tr at end of repeat, 1 ss into 2nd of 2 ch.

2nd to 8th row As 2nd row of neck edging. Fasten off.

51

Jumper

Materials

10 (11, 12) oz Coats *Carefree Bri-Nylon*
3 ply
Milward Disc (aluminium) crochet hook
3·50 (no. 9).

Measurements

To fit 34 (37, 40) in. [86 (94, 100) cm] bust
Length at centre back 24 (24½, 24½) in. [36
(62, 62) cm]
Sleeve seam 13½ (14, 14) in. [34 (35, 35) cm]

Tension

1 repeat of pattern to 1⅝ in. [41 mm].

Tension check

Before you crochet this design check the

tension by working an approximate 3 in.
[76 mm] square in the stitch pattern (22 ch
and 16 rows). If your tension is loose use a
size finer hook, if tight use a size larger
hook.

Back

Commence with 112 (122, 132) ch worked
loosely.

1st row 1 dc into 2nd ch from hook, 1 dc
into each ch, 1 ch, turn.

2nd row 1 dc into each of first 3 dc, * 3 ch,
miss 2 dc, 1 tr into next dc, 3 ch, miss 2 dc,
1 dc into each of next 5 dc; repeat from *
omitting 2 dc at end of last repeat, 1 ch,
turn.

3rd row 1 dc into each of first 2 dc, * 3 ch,
miss 2 ch, 1 dc into each of next 3 sts, 3 ch,
miss next dc, 1 dc into each of next 3 dc;
repeat from * omitting 1 dc at end of last
repeat, 6 ch, turn.

4th row * Miss 2 ch, 1 dc into each of next 5
sts, 3 ch, miss next dc, 1 tr into next dc, 3 ch;
repeat from * omitting 3 ch at end of last
repeat, 1 ch, turn.

5th row 1 dc into each of first 2 sts, * 3 ch,
miss next dc, 1 dc into each of next 3 dc, 3
ch, miss 2 ch, 1 dc into each of next 3 sts;
repeat from * omitting 1 dc at end of last
repeat, 1 ch, turn.

6th row 1 dc into each of first 3 sts, * 3 ch,
miss next dc, 1 tr into next dc, 3 ch, miss 2
ch, 1 dc into each of next 5 sts; repeat from
* omitting 2 dc at end of last repeat, 1 ch,
turn.

Last 4 rows form pattern.
Repeat pattern until work measures 15 in.
(or length required) ending with a 5th pattern row and omitting turning ch at end of
last row.

Armhole shaping
1st size only

1st row 1 ss into each of first 12 sts, 1 dc into each of next 3 sts, * 3 ch, miss next dc, 1 tr into next dc, 3 ch, miss 2 ch, 1 dc into each of next 5 sts; repeat from * 8 times more omitting 2 dc at end of last repeat, 1 ch, turn.

2nd and 3rd sizes only

1st row 1 ss into each of first 19 sts, 6 ch, * miss 2 ch, 1 dc into each of next 5 sts, 3 ch, miss next dc, 1 tr into next dc, 3 ch; repeat from * 8 (9) times more, omitting 3 ch at end of last repeat, 1 ch, turn.

All sizes

Keeping continuity of pattern work until armhole measures $7\frac{1}{2}$ (8, 8) in. [19 (20, 20) cm] or length required ending with a 6th pattern row and omitting turning ch at end of last row.

Shoulder shaping

1st row 1 ss into each of first 11 sts, 1 dc into each of next 3 dc, 3 ch and continue in pattern to within last 11 sts, turn.

2nd row 1 ss into each of first 9 sts, 1 dc into next ch, 3 ch, miss next dc, 1 tr into next dc and continue in pattern to within last 9 sts, turn.

3rd row 1 ss into each of first 10 (10, 16) sts, 1 dc into each of next 2 sts, 3 ch and continue in pattern to within last 10 (10, 16) sts. Fasten off.

Front

Work as Back until armhole measures $3\frac{1}{2}$ in. [88 mm] ending with a 5th pattern row.

Right neck shaping
1st and 2nd sizes only

1st row 1 dc into each of first 3 sts, (3 ch, 54

miss next dc, 1 tr into next dc, 3 ch, miss 2 ch, 1 dc into each of next 5 sts) twice, 3 ch, miss next dc, 1 tr into next dc, 1 ch, turn.

3rd size only

1st row 1 dc into each of first 3 sts, (3 ch, miss next dc, 1 tr into next dc, 3 ch, miss 2 ch, 1 dc into each of next 5 sts) 3 times, omitting 2 dc at end of last repeat, 1 ch, turn.

All sizes

Continue in pattern until armhole measures same as Back, ending at neck edge.

Shoulder shaping

1st row Continue in pattern to within last 11 sts, turn.

2nd row 1 ss into each of first 9 sts, 1 dc into next ch, 3 ch and continue in pattern to end. Fasten off.

Left neck shaping
1st and 2nd sizes only

1st row Miss 23 dc at centre front, attach yarn to next dc, 6 ch, miss 2 ch, 1 dc into each of next 5 sts, 3 ch and continue in pattern to end of row.

3rd size only

1st row Miss 23 dc at centre front, attach yarn to next dc, 1 dc into same place as join, 1 dc into each of next 2 sts, 3 ch, miss next dc, 1 tr into next dc, 3 ch and continue in pattern to end of row.

All sizes

Continue until armhole measures same as Back keeping neck edge straight and omitting turning ch at end of last row (armhole edge).

Shoulder shaping

Work to correspond with other side.

Sleeves

Commence with 62 ch and work as Back for first 6 rows.

7th row * 2 dc into first dc (inc made), 1 dc into next dc, 3 ch, and continue in pattern ending with 2 dc into last dc (another inc made), 3 ch, turn.

8th row Miss first dc, 1 tr into next dc, 3 ch and continue in pattern ending with 1 tr into each of last 2 dc, 1 ch, turn.

9th row 1 dc into each of first 3 sts, 3 ch and continue in pattern ending with 1 dc into each of last 3 sts, 1 ch, turn.

10th row 1 dc into each of first 4 sts, 3 ch and continue in pattern ending with 1 dc into each of last 4 sts, 1 ch, turn.

11th row 2 dc into first dc, 1 dc into each of next 2 sts, 3 ch and continue in pattern ending with 1 dc into each of last 3 sts, 1 dc into same place as last dc, 1 ch, turn.

12th row 1 dc into first dc, 3 ch, miss next dc, 1 tr into next dc, 3 ch and continue in pattern ending with 3 ch, 1 dc into last dc, 1 ch, turn.

13th row 1 dc into first dc, 3 ch, miss 2 ch, 1 dc into each of next 3 sts and continue in pattern ending with 3 ch, 1 dc into last dc, 6 ch, turn.

14th row Miss first dc and 2 ch, 1 dc into each of next 5 sts, 3 ch and continue in pattern ending with 3 ch, 1 tr into last dc, 1 ch, turn.

Work in pattern without shaping for 10 rows more. * Repeat from * to * twice more.

For 3rd size only

Repeat 7th to 14th row once more.

Continue without shaping until work measures approximately $14\frac{1}{2}$ ($15\frac{1}{2}$, $15\frac{1}{2}$) in. [36 (39, 39) cm] (or length required) ending with a 3rd or 5th pattern row and omit-

ting turning ch at end of last row. Fasten off.

To make up

Do not press. Join shoulder and side seams. Join sleeve seams to within $1\frac{1}{2}$ (2, 2) in. [38 (50, 50) mm] from top. Sew sleeves in position.

Lower edging

1st row With right side facing attach yarn to side seam, 4 ch, * miss 1 st, 1 tr into next st, 1 ch; repeat from * all round ending with 1 ss into 3rd of 4 ch.

2nd and 3rd rows 1 dc into same place as ss, 1 dc into each st, 1 ss into first dc.

4th row Do not turn but continue to work a row of dc in reverse as follows. 1 dc into last dc worked * 1 dc into previous dc; repeat from * ending with 1 dc into same place as ss, 1 ss into first dc. Fasten off.

Sleeve edgings

Attach yarn at seam and work as Lower edging.

Neck edging

1st row With right side facing attach yarn to left shoulder seam and work an even number of dc neatly all round ending with 1 ss into first dc.

2nd row 1 dc into same place as ss, * 1 dc into each dc to within dc at next corner, miss corner dc; repeat from * once more, 1 dc into each dc, 1 ss into first dc.

3rd row 4 ch, * miss next dc, 1 tr into next dc, 1 ch; repeat from * omitting 1 ch at each corner, 1 ss into 3rd of 4 ch.

4th to 6th row As 2nd to 4th row of Lower edging.

Star stitch jacket

Materials

18 (19, 20) oz Coats *Carefree Bri-Nylon*
4 ply
Milward Disc (aluminium) crochet hook
4·00 (no. 8)
5 buttons
1 snap fastener

Measurements

To fit 34 (36, 38) in. [86 (92, 96) cm] bust
Length at centre back 22 (22½, 23) in. [56
(57, 58) cm]
Sleeve seam 17½ in. [44 cm]

Tension

3 rows and 3 stars to 1 square in. [25 mm].

Tension check

Before you crochet this design check the
tension by working a 3 in. [76 mm] square
in the stitch pattern (23 ch and 9 rows). If
your tension is loose use a size finer hook,
if tight use a size larger hook.

Back

Commence with 109 (115, 121) ch.

1st row Miss first ch, ★ insert hook into
next ch, draw yarn through, ★; repeat from
★ to ★ 4 times more (6 lps on hook), yarn
over and draw through all lps on hook, 1 ch
to form eye (star made), ★★ insert hook
into eye at top of star just made and draw
yarn through, insert hook into back of last
lp of same star and draw yarn through,
insert hook into same ch as last lp of same
star and draw yarn through; repeat from ★
to ★ twice (6 lps on hook), yarn over and
draw through all lps on hook, 1 ch (another
star made); repeat from ★★ to last ch, 1 dc
into last ch, 3 ch, turn.

56

2nd row Miss first ch from hook, draw yarn through each of next 2 ch, next dc, then through eye at top of first star and through next st (6 lps on hook), yarn over and draw through all lps on hook, 1 ch, * draw yarn through eye at top of star just made, through back of last lp of same star, through same st as last lp of same star, through eye at top of next star and through next st (6 lps on hook), yarn over and draw through all lps on hook, 1 ch (star made over star); repeat from * ending with 1 dc into extreme end of row, 3 ch, turn.

2nd row forms pattern.

Continue in pattern until work measures 14½ in. [37 cm] (or length required), omitting turning ch at end of last row, turn.

Armhole shaping

1st row 1 ss into each of first 5 sts, * 2 ch, draw yarn through eye at top of next star and through next st, yarn over and draw through all lps on hook, 1 ch (hlf star made), star over each star to within last 2 stars, 2 ch, turn.

2nd row Miss first star and work a hlf star over next star, star over each star, 2 ch, turn.

3rd row As 2nd row working 1 dc into last st.

Continue in pattern until armhole measures 7½ (8, 8½) in. [19 (20, 21) cm] omitting turning ch at end of last row.

Neck and shoulder shaping

1st row 1 ss into each of first 9 sts, 2 ch and complete a hlf star, star over each of next 11 (12, 13) stars, 2 ch, turn.

2nd row Miss first star and work a hlf star over next star, star over each of next 4 (5, 6) stars, 1 ss into next st. Fasten off.

Miss 13 (14, 15) stars, rejoin yarn to 2nd st of next star and work to correspond with first side.

Right front

Commence with 65 (69, 73) ch and work as Back to armhole shaping.

Armhole shaping

1st row Pattern to within last 2 stars, 2 ch, turn.

2nd row Miss first star, work a hlf star over next star, pattern to end.

3rd row Pattern to within hlf star, 1 dc into top of hlf star, 3 ch, turn.

Continue in pattern without shaping until armhole measures 5½ (6, 6½) in. [14 (15, 16) cm], ending at front edge. Fasten off.

Neck shaping

1st row Miss 6 (7, 8) stars at front edge, join yarn to 2nd st of next star, 2 ch and work hlf star as before, pattern to end.

2nd row Star over each of first 18 (19, 20) stars, 2 ch, turn.

3rd row Miss first star, work hlf star over next star, pattern to end.

4th row Star over each of first 16 (17, 18) stars, 2 ch, turn.

5th row As 3rd row.

6th row Star over each of first 14 (15, 16) stars, 1 dc into last st, 3 ch, turn.

Shoulder shaping

1st row Star over each of first 10 (11, 12) stars, 1 ss into next st, turn.

2nd row Miss ss, 1 ss into each of next 8 sts, 2 ch and work a hlf star, pattern to end. Fasten off.

Left front

Work as Right front, reversing all shapings.

Sleeves

Commence with 51 (55, 59) ch.

1st row As 1st row on Back.

2nd row Work in pattern ending with—draw yarn through eye at top of last star made, through back of last lp of same star, through st at extreme end of row, yarn over and draw through all lps on hook (an inc made), 3 ch, turn.

3rd row Miss first ch from hook, draw yarn through each of next 2 ch, through top of hlf star and through next st (5 lps on hook), yarn over and draw through all lps on hook, 1 ch (star made over inc), pattern to end, working inc as on previous row.

4th row As 3rd row, omitting inc at end of row, 1 dc into last st, 3 ch, turn.

Work in pattern for 3 rows.
Repeat last 6 rows 7 times more, then 2nd to 4th row again ending last row with 2 ch, turn.

Top shaping

1st row Work hlf star as before, star over each of next 39 (41, 43) stars, hlf star over next star, 2 ch, turn.

2nd row Miss hlf star, hlf star over next star, star over each of next 37 (39, 41) stars, hlf star over next star, 2 ch, turn.

Repeat last row 7 times more, having 2 stars less on each row, ending last row with 3 ch, turn.

10th row Miss hlf star and eye at top of next star, draw yarn through each of next 3 sts, yarn over and draw through all lps on hook, 1 ch, work 19 (21, 23) stars, 1 ch, miss eye of next star, hlf star over next 3 sts, 3 ch, turn.

Repeat last row twice more, having 4 stars less on each row, omitting turning ch at end of last row.

13th row 1 ss into each of first 6 sts, hlf star over next 2 sts, work 3 (5, 7) stars, hlf star over next 2 sts, 1 ss into next st. Fasten off.

Collar

Commence with 109 (111, 113) ch and work as Back for 7 rows. Fasten off.

Edging

1st row Attach yarn to foundation ch and work a row of dc all round collar, having 3 dc into same place at each corner and ending with 1 ss into first dc.

2nd row 1 dc into each dc, working 3 dc into centre dc of each corner, 1 ss into first dc. Fasten off.

To make up

Do not press. Sew shoulder, side and sleeve seams and set in sleeves.

Edging

1st row Attach yarn to any st at side seam and work a row of dc all round jacket, having 3 dc into same place at each corner and ending with 1 ss into first dc.

2nd row 1 dc into each dc, working 3 dc into centre dc at each corner, 1 ss into first dc. Fasten off.

Work round sleeve edge to correspond.
Sew on collar.
Sew buttons to left front and make buttonholes through eyes of stars on right front to correspond, buttonhole stitch round holes if required.
Sew snap fastener at neck edge.
Press all seams lightly on the wrong side with a cool iron.

Poncho

Materials

5 oz Coats *Cadenza Courtelle* 4 ply main
colour
2 oz contrasting colour
2 oz second contrasting colour
2 oz third contrasting colour
1 Milward Disc crochet hook 4·00 (no. 8)

Measurements

Length at centre front 23 in. [58 cm],
excluding fringe

Tension

1 shell and 1 dc to $1\frac{1}{4}$ in. [32 mm].
4 rows to $1\frac{1}{2}$ in. [38 mm].

Main section

Using M commence with 96 ch and being careful not to twist, join with a ss to form a ring.

1st row 1 dc into same place as ss, * miss 2 ch, 5 tr into next ch—a shell made, miss 2 ch, 1 dc into next ch; repeat from * omitting 1 dc at end of last repeat, 1 ss into first dc. 16 shells.

2nd row 5 ch, a shell into same place as ss, (miss 2 tr, 1 dc into next tr, dc made over shell, a shell into next dc) 8 times, 2 ch, a shell into same place as last shell, (1 dc over next shell, a shell into next dc) 7 times, 1 dc over next shell, 4 tr into same place as first shell, 1 ss into 3rd of 5 ch. 18 shells.

3rd row 1 ss into 2 ch sp, 5 ch, a shell into 2 ch sp, * 1 dc over next shell, a shell into next dc; repeat from * to next 2 ch sp, ending with 1 dc over next shell, into next 2 ch sp work a shell 2 ch and a shell; repeat from first * omitting a shell 2 ch and a shell at end of last repeat, 4 tr into 2 ch sp, 1 ss into 3rd of 5 ch. Fasten off.

4th row Attach C to 2 ch sp, 5 ch, and complete as 3rd row.

5th and 6th rows As 3rd row.

Fasten off at end of 6th row.

7th to 9th row Using SC work as 4th to 6th row.

10th to 12th row Using TC work as 4th to 6th row.

13th to 15th row Using M work as 4th to 6th row.

Repeat 4th to 15th row once more, then 4th to 9th row again.

Neck edging

Attach M to base of any shell on 1st row, 1 dc into same place as join, * 1 shell into base of shell on 2nd row, 1 dc into base of shell on 1st row; repeat from *, 1 ss into first dc. Fasten off.

Lower edging

Attach M to any 2 ch sp, ** 1 dc 2 ch and 1 dc into 2 ch sp, 2 ch, miss 1 tr, 1 dc into next tr, * 2 ch, miss 1 tr, 1 dc into next tr, 2 ch, miss 1 tr 1 dc and 1 tr, 1 dc into next tr; repeat from * to next 2 ch sp, ending with 2 ch, miss 1 tr, 1 dc into next tr, 2 ch; repeat from ** ending with 1 ss into first dc. Fasten off.

Fringe

Cut M into 15 in. lengths.
Using crochet hook, take 5 strands of yarn and loop into each 2 ch sp on Lower edging, then taking 5 strands from each group knot them together 1 in. from top.

Do not press.

Stole

Materials

13 oz Coats *Carefree Bri-Nylon* 4 ply
Milward Disc (aluminium) crochet hook
4·00 (no. 8)

Measurements

Width 20 in. [50 cm]
Length 60 in. [152 cm]

Tension

4 rows to 1½ in. [38 mm] and 5 sts to 1 in.
[25 mm].

Tension check

Before you crochet this design check the
tension by working an approximate 3 in.
[76 mm] square in the stitch pattern (15 ch
and 8 rows). If your tension is loose use a
finer hook, if tight use a size larger hook.

Commence with 111 ch.

1st row 1 tr into 4th ch from hook, 1 tr into
each ch, 3 ch, turn.

2nd row Miss first tr, 1 tr into each tr, 1 tr
into top of turning ch, 4 ch, turn.

3rd row Leaving the last loop of each on

hook work 3 dbl tr into first tr, thread over
and draw through all loops on hook (a 3
dbl tr cluster made), * 5 ch, miss 2 tr, 1 dc
into next tr, 5 ch, miss 2 tr, a 4 dbl tr cluster
into next tr; repeat from * working last
cluster into 3rd of 3 ch, 1 ch, turn.

4th row 1 dc into top of first cluster, * 5 ch,
1 dc into next cluster; repeat from * ending
with 3 ch, turn.

5th row * 5 tr into next sp, 1 tr into next dc;
repeat from * ending with 3 ch, turn.

6th row As 2nd row.

Repeat 3rd to 6th row until work measures
approximately 60 in. [152 cm] or length
required, ending with a 6th pattern row.
Fasten off.

Edging

Cut a piece of cardboard a little deeper
than required depth of fringe, wind yarn
round four times. Cut along one side.
Double the lengths of yarn. Insert hook
between first and second treble on short
end of stole. Pull through the doubled yarn
forming a loop on hook. Through this loop
draw ends of yarn. Tighten knot. Repeat
leaving two trebles between each fringe
knot. Trim edges of fringe evenly.

Washing instructions

Wash frequently and avoid over-soiling.

Stole

Materials

5 oz Coats *Cadenza Courtelle* 4 ply
Milward Disc (aluminium) crochet hook
4·50 (no. 7)

Measurements

Long edge 58½ in. [150 cm]
Short edges 31½ in. [80 cm] (excluding
fringe)

Tension

Size of motif 4½ in. [114 mm] square.
If your tension is loose use a size finer hook,
if tight use a size larger hook.

First strip

First motif

Commence with 5 ch.

1st row (right side) Yarn over, insert hook
into 5th ch from hook, draw yarn up
approximately ½ in. [13 mm], yarn over
and complete as tr (all tr worked in this
manner), into same ch work 1 tr, 3 ch
(3 tr, 3 ch) twice and 2 tr, leaving the last
lp of each on hook work 1 tr into same
place as last tr and 1 tr into 5th of 5 ch,
yarn over and draw through all lps on
hook—a joint st made, 1 ss into sp just
formed, 4 ch, turn.

2nd row 2 tr into same sp as last ss, (2 ch,
into next sp work 3 tr 3 ch and 3 tr) 3 times,
2 ch, 2 tr into next sp, a joint st into same sp
and 4th of 4 ch, 1 ss into sp just formed, 4
ch, turn.

3rd row 2 tr into same sp as last ss, * 2 ch, 3
tr into next sp, 2 ch, into next sp work 3 tr 3
ch and 3 tr; repeat from * twice more, 2 ch,
3 tr into next sp, 2 ch, 2 tr into next sp, a
joint st into same sp and 4th of 4 ch, 1 ss
into sp just formed, 4 ch, turn.

4th row 2 tr into same sp as last ss, * (2 ch,
3 tr into next sp) twice, 2 ch, into next
sp work 3 tr 3 ch and 3 tr; repeat from * 3
times more, omitting 3 tr at end of last
repeat, 1 ss into 4th of 4 ch. Fasten off.

Second motif

Work as first motif, ending 4th row with 1
ch, turn.

Joining

1 ch, turn, 1 dc into last sp made, 2 ch, 1 dc
into corresponding sp on first motif, * 2 ch,
1 dc into centre tr of next 3 tr on second
motif, 2 ch, 1 dc into corresponding tr on
first motif, 2 ch, 1 dc into next sp on second
motif, 2 ch, 1 dc into corresponding sp on
first motif; repeat from * 3 times more.
Fasten off.

Make 4 more motifs joining each as second
motif was joined to first, placing as shown
on diagram.

Half motif

Commence with 6 ch.

1st row Into 6th ch from hook work 3 tr 3 ch and 3 tr, 1 ch, 1 tr into same place as last tr, 5 ch, turn.

2nd row 3 tr into next sp, 2 ch, into next sp work 3 tr 3 ch and 3 tr, 2 ch, 3 tr into next sp, 1 ch, 1 tr into 5th of 6 ch, 5 ch, turn.

3rd row (3 tr into next sp, 2 ch) twice, into next sp work 3 tr 3 ch and 3 tr, (2 ch, 3 tr into next sp) twice, 1 ch, 1 tr into 4th of 5 ch, 5 ch, turn.

4th row (3 tr into next sp, 2 ch) 3 times, into next sp work 3 tr 3 ch and 3 tr, (2 ch, 3 tr into next sp) 3 times, 1 ch, 1 tr into 4th of 5 ch, 1 ch, turn, join to last motif as before.

Make 6 more strips as before, having one motif less on each strip, last strip consisting of one half motif, and omitting joining at end of last half motif (see diagram).

Joining of strips

Place strips as shown on diagram and join as follows:

With right side of first strip facing, attach yarn to first dc on last joining, 2 ch, 1 dc into first sp on half motif on next strip, 2 ch, 1 dc into first sp on next motif on first strip * (2 ch, 1 dc into centre tr of next 3 tr on next strip, 2 ch, 1 dc into corresponding tr on first strip, 2 ch, 1 dc into next sp on next strip, 2 ch, 1 dc into corresponding sp on first strip) twice, 2 ch, 1 dc into centre tr of next 3 tr on next strip, 2 ch, 1 dc into corresponding tr on first strip, 2 ch, 1 ss into dc in next sp on next strip, 2 ch, 1 ss into corresponding dc on first strip, 2 ch, 1 ss into dc in next sp on next strip, 2 ch, 1 ss into corresponding dc on first strip—a joining made over joining; repeat from * omitting a joining over joining at end of last repeat, 1 dc into next sp on next strip, 2 ch, 1 dc into corresponding sp on first strip. Fasten off.

Join other strips to correspond.

Edging

1st row With wrong side facing, attach yarn to last tr worked on half motif of last strip (see * on diagram), 1 dc into same place as join, work dc evenly over row-ends of half motifs on long edge of stole, 1 ch, turn.

2nd row 1 dc into each dc. Fasten off.

Fringe

Cut yarn into 9 in. [23 cm] lengths. Using crochet hook, take 5 strands of yarn and loop into sps on the two short sides.

Do not press.

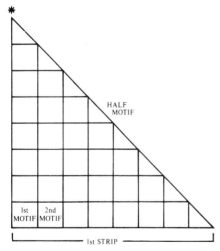

*

HALF MOTIF

1st MOTIF 2nd MOTIF

1st STRIP

Collar and cuffs

Materials

1 oz Coats *Carefree Bri-Nylon* 3 ply
Milward Disc (aluminium) crochet hook
3·50 (no. 9)

Measurements

Depth of collar and cuffs 2½ in. [64 mm]
Length of collar round neck 19 in. [74 cm]
Length of cuff round lower edge 9 in. [229
mm]

Tension

6 tr to 1 in. [25 mm].

Tension check

Before you crochet this design check your
tension by working a 2½ in. [64 mm] square
in the stitch pattern (17 ch and 5 rows). If
your tension is loose use a size finer hook;
if tight use a larger hook.

Collar

Commence with 111 ch, or length required.

1st row 1 tr into 4th ch from hook, 1 tr into
each ch, 1 ch, turn.

2nd row Miss first tr, 1 dc into each tr, 1 dc
into top of turning ch, 5 ch, turn.

3rd row Miss first dc, 1 trip tr into each dc,
1 trip tr into top of turning ch, 5 ch, turn.

4th row Miss first trip tr, 1 trip tr into each
trip tr, 1 trip tr into top of turning ch, 12 ch,
turn.

5th row 1 dc into 7th ch from hook (picot
made), miss first trip tr, * 1 trip tr into next
trip tr, 7 ch, 1 dc into top of last trip tr;
repeat from * to end, 1 trip tr into top of
turning ch, 7 ch, 1 dc into top of last trip tr.
Fasten off.

Cuffs (make two)

Commence with 57 ch, or length required
and work as for collar.

Full length stockings

Materials

5 oz Coats *Carefree Bri-Nylon* 3 ply
Milward Disc (aluminium) crochet hook
3·50 (no. 9)

Measurements

To fit a 9 to 10½ in. [229 to 267 mm] foot
To fit leg length 30 to 33 in. [76 to 83 cm]

Tension

2 pattern rows to ½ in. [13 mm] approximately.

Heel

Commence at base of heel with 14 ch.

1st row 1 tr into 7th ch from hook, 1 tr into each of next 7 ch, 4 ch, now working along opposite side of foundation ch work 1 tr into each of next 7 sts, 1 ss into 3rd of 7 ch.

2nd row 3 ch, ★ into next sp work 2 tr 2 ch and 2 tr, 1 tr into each tr; repeat from ★ ending with 1 ss into 3rd of 3 ch.

3rd row 3 ch, ★ 1 tr into each tr, into sp work 2 tr 2 ch and 2 tr; repeat from ★ ending with 1 ss into 3rd of 3 ch.

4th to 6th row Work in same manner as 3rd row, having 8 tr more on each row and having 56 tr on 6th row. Fasten off.

Toe

Commence with 10 ch.

1st row 1 tr into 7th ch from hook, 1 tr into each of next 3 ch, 4 ch, now work along opposite side of foundation ch, 1 tr into each of next 3 ch, 1 ss into 3rd of 7 ch.

2nd row 3 ch, ★ into sp work 2 tr 2 ch and 2 tr, 1 tr into each tr; repeat from ★ ending with 1 ss into 3rd of 3 ch.

3rd row 3 ch, 1 tr into each of next 2 tr, ★ into sp work 2 tr 2 ch and 2 tr, 1 tr into each tr; repeat from ★ ending with 1 ss into 3rd of 3 ch.

4th row Work in same manner as 3rd row (32 tr).

5th row 3 ch, 1 tr into each tr, into sp work 4 tr, 1 tr into each tr, into sp work 4 tr, 1 tr into each tr, 1 ss into 3rd of 3 ch (40 tr).

6th to 8th row 3 ch, 1 tr into each tr, 1 ss into 3rd of 3 ch. Do not fasten off.

Foot

1st row 5 ch, 1 dbl tr into same place as ss, * 2 ch, miss next tr, 1 dc into next tr, 2 ch, miss next tr, into next tr work 1 dbl tr 1 ch and 1 dbl tr (V st made); repeat from * omitting V st at end of last repeat, 1 ss into 4th of 5 ch.

2nd row 1 dc into 1 ch sp, * 2 ch, V st into next dc, 2 ch, 1 dc into next 1 ch sp; repeat from * omitting 1 dc at end of last repeat, 1 ss into first dc.

3rd row 5 ch, 1 dbl tr into same place as ss, * 2 ch, 1 dc into next 1 ch sp, 2 ch, V st into next dc; repeat from * omitting V st at end of last repeat, 1 ss into 4th of 5 ch.

2nd and 3rd rows form pattern. Repeat pattern until work measures 6½ in. [165 mm] or length required, ending with a 2nd row. Fasten off.

Heel joining

1st row Attach yarn to 8th dc worked on last row, 1 dc into same place as join, 2 ch, with wrong side facing work 1 dc into 2 ch sp at side of Heel, 2 ch, 1 dc into next 1 ch sp on Foot, 2 ch, miss next 3 sts on Heel, * 1 dc into next st, 2 ch, 1 dc into next dc on Foot, 2 ch, miss next 2 sts on Heel, 1 dc into next st, 2 ch, 1 dc into next 1 ch sp on Foot, ** 2 ch, miss next 2 sts on Heel; repeat from * 3 times more ending at **, 2 ch, miss next 3 sts on Heel, 1 dc into 2 ch sp at side of Heel, 2 ch, 1 ss into next dc on Foot (one side of Heel joined). Now continue thus: 5 ch, 1 dbl tr into same place as ss, (2 ch, 1 dc into next 1 ch sp, 2 ch, V st into next dc) 5 times, 2 ch, 1 dc into 2 ch sp at side of Heel. Continue working along unformed side of Heel as follows: 2 ch, miss next tr (V st into next st, 2 ch, miss 1 st, 1 dc into next st, 2 ch, miss 1 st) 6 times, V st into next st,

2 ch, 1 dc into 2 ch sp at side of Heel, 2 ch, 1 ss into 4th of 5 ch.

Next row 1 dc into 1 ch sp, V st into next dc, (2 ch, 1 dc into next 1 ch sp, 2 ch, V st into next dc) 3 times, 2 ch, 1 dc into next 1 ch sp, 2 ch, V st into next dc, 1 dc into next 1 ch sp, 2 ch, miss next dc, 1 dc into next 1 ch sp (a decrease made), (2 ch, V st into next dc, 2 ch, 1 dc into next 1 ch sp) 6 times, miss next dc, 1 hlf tr into first dc (another decrease made).

Next row 5 ch, 1 dbl tr into sp just formed (2 ch, 1 dc into next 1 ch sp, 2 ch, V st into next dc) 4 times, 2 ch, 1 dc into next 1 ch sp, 2 ch, miss next dc, V st into next sp, (2 ch, 1 dc into next 1 ch sp, 2 ch, V st into next dc) 5 times, 2 ch, 1 dc into next 1 ch sp, 2 ch, 1 ss into 4th of 5 ch.

Repeat 2 pattern rows 13 times more, then work 2nd row again.

Leg shaping

1st row As 3rd pattern row but working 3 ch lps in place of 2 ch lps.

2nd row As 2nd pattern row but working 3 ch lps in place of 2 ch lps.

Repeat last 2 rows 22 times more or length required ending with a 2nd row.

Stocking top

1st row 1 ss into lp, 4 ch, 1 dbl tr into same lp, * 2 dbl tr into 1 ch sp, (2 dbl tr into 3 ch lp) twice; repeat from * omitting 2 dbl tr at end of last repeat, 1 ss into 4th of 4 ch.

2nd to 4th row 4 ch, 1 dbl tr into each dbl tr, 1 ss into 4th of 4 ch. Fasten off.

Work another stocking in same manner.

Beaded beret

Materials

1 ball Coats *Cadenza Courtelle* 4 ply
2 balls Coats *Cadenza Courtelle* double knitting
Milward Disc (aluminium) crochet hooks 3·00 (no. 11) and 4·00 (no. 8) (if your crochet is loose use size finer hooks, if tight use size larger hooks)
258 light-weight beads with holes large enough to take smaller size of crochet hook

Measurement

To fit average head

Tension

First 2 rows of lining 1½ in. [38 mm] in diameter.

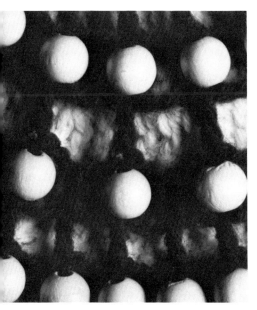

Beaded section

Using 4 ply and 3·00 (no. 11) hook, commence with 6 ch, join with a ss to form a ring.

1st row 12 dc into ring, 1 ss into first dc.

2nd row 6 ch, * insert hook through bead and into next dc and draw yarn through bead (2 lps on hook), thread over and draw through both lps on hook (B st made), 3 ch, 1 tr into next dc, 3 ch; repeat from * omitting 1 tr and 3 ch at end of last repeat, 1 ss into 3rd of 6 ch.

3rd row 7 ch, * 1 tr into next B st, 4 ch, 1 tr into next tr, 4 ch; repeat from * omitting 1 tr and 4 ch at end of last repeat, 1 ss into 3rd of 7 ch.

4th row Insert hook through bead and complete B st in same place as ss, * 3 ch, 1 tr into next sp, 3 ch, B st into next tr; repeat from * omitting B st at end of last repeat, 1 ss into first B st.

5th row 7 ch, * 1 tr into next tr, 4 ch, 1 tr into next B st, 4 ch; repeat from * omitting 1 tr and 4 ch at end of last repeat, 1 ss into 3rd of 7 ch.

6th row B st into same place as ss, * 4 ch, B st into next tr; repeat from * ending with 4 ch, 1 ss into first B st.

7th row 9 ch, * 1 tr into next B st, 6 ch; repeat from * ending with 1 ss into 3rd of 9 ch.

8th row As 4th row.

9th row 6 ch, * 1 tr into next tr, 3 ch, 1 tr into next B st, 3 ch; repeat from * omitting 1 tr and 3 ch at end of last repeat, 1 ss into 3rd of 6 ch.

Repeat 6th to 9th row once more.

14th row Insert hook through bead and complete B st in same place as ss, * 4 ch, 1 tr into next tr, 4 ch, B st into next tr; repeat from * omitting B st at end of last repeat, 1 ss into first B st.

15th row 9 ch, * 1 tr into next B st, 6 ch;

repeat from * ending with 1 ss into 3rd of 9 ch.

16th row As 4th row. Fasten off.

Lining

Using double knitting and 4·00 (no. 8) hook, commence with 4 ch, join with a ss to form a ring.

1st row 8 dc into ring, 1 ss into first dc.

2nd row 3 ch, 1 tr into same place as ss, 2 tr into each dc, 1 ss into 3rd of 3 ch (16 sts).

3rd row 3 ch, 1 tr into same place as ss, 2 tr into each tr 1 ss into 3rd of 3 ch (32 sts).

4th row 3 ch, 1 tr into same place as ss, 1 tr into next tr, * 2 tr into next tr, 1 tr into next tr; repeat from * ending with 1 ss into 3rd of 3 ch (48 sts).

Continue in this manner for 8 rows more increasing 12 tr evenly spaced on each row (144 sts).

13th to 15th row 3 ch, 1 tr into each tr, 1 ss into 3rd of 3 ch. Fasten off.

Place wrong sides of each section together.

Band

1st row With right side of lining facing, using double knitting and 4·00 (no. 8) hook, insert hook into any st on lining and through any sp of last row on beaded section and draw lp through, thread over and draw through all lps on hook (a joining dc made), * a joining dc into next st on lining and next sp on beaded section, miss next st on lining, a joining dc into next st on lining and next sp on beaded section; repeat from * omitting 1 joining dc at end of last repeat, 1 ss into first joining dc.

2nd to 6th row 1 dc into each dc, 1 ss into first dc, ending last row with 1 ch, turn.

7th row 1 dc into each dc, 1 ss into first dc. Fasten off.

Handbag

Materials

2 oz Coats *Cadenza Courtelle* double knitting main colour
2 oz first contrasting colour
2 oz second contrasting colour
Milward Disc crochet hook 4·50 (no. 7)
$\frac{2}{3}$ yd [61 cm] lining 36 in. [92 cm cm] wide
$\frac{1}{2}$ yd [46 cm] heavy *Vilene* 32 in. [80 cm] wide
Cardboard for base
Bag frame with 9 in. [229 mm] rods

Measurements

$9\frac{1}{2}$ in. $\times$ $9\frac{1}{2}$ in. $\times$ $3\frac{1}{2}$ in. [241 $\times$ 241 $\times$ 89 mm] approximately.

Tension

First 3 rows to $1\frac{1}{2}$ in. [38 mm].
3 puff sts to $1\frac{3}{4}$ in. [44 mm].

Main section

First side

Using M commence with 52 ch.

1st row 1 tr into 4th ch from hook, 1 tr into each of next 3 ch, * 1 ch, miss 1 ch, 1 tr into each of next 2 ch; repeat from * 13 times more, 1 tr into each of next 3 ch. Fasten off.

2nd row With right side of tr facing attach C to ch before first tr on previous row, 3 ch, 1 tr into each of next 2 tr, * 1 ch, yarn over

hook, insert hook into next sp and draw lp up $\frac{5}{8}$ in. [16 mm], (yarn over hook, insert hook into same place and draw yarn through as before) 3 times, yarn over and draw through all lps on hook, 1 ch to fasten (a puff st made); repeat from * 13 times more, 1 ch, 1 tr into each of last 3 tr. Fasten off.

3rd row With right side facing attach SC to 3rd of first 3 ch on previous row, 3 ch, 1 tr into each of next 2 tr, * a puff st into next sp, 1 ch; repeat from * 13 times more, puff st into next sp, 1 tr into each of next 3 tr. Fasten off.

4th row As 2nd row.

5th row With right side facing attach M to 3rd of first 3 ch on previous row, 3 ch, 1 tr into each of next 2 tr, * 2 tr into next sp, 1 ch; repeat from * 13 times more, 2 tr into next sp, 1 tr into each of last 3 tr. Fasten off.

6th row Using SC work as 2nd row.

7th row Using C work as 3rd row.

8th row Using SC work as 2nd row.

9th row As 5th row.

Repeat 2nd to 9th row once more, then 2nd to 8th row again.

Top edge

1st row With right side facing miss first 2 sts on previous row, attach M to front half of next st, 3 ch, 1 tr into front half of each st to within last 3 sts, 3 ch, ss into front half of next st, turn. 45 sts.

2nd row Working into other half of each st, 1 dc into same st as last ss, 1 dc into each st, 1 ch, turn.

3rd row To form a sp for rod work 1 dc into each dc on 2nd row and into base of each tr on 1st row.

Next row (edging) With right side facing attach M to first dc on previous row, 1 dc into same place as join, * 3 ch, 3 tr into same place as last dc, miss 3 dc, 1 dc into next dc; repeat from * to end. Fasten off.

Second side

1st row With right side facing attach C to base of last tr made on 1st row of First side, 3 ch, 1 tr into each of next 2 tr, * 1 ch, a puff st into next sp; repeat from * 13 times more, 1 ch, 1 tr into base of last 3 sts. Fasten off. Repeat from 3rd row to end of First side.

Gusset (make 2)

Using M commence with 20 ch.

1st row 1 tr into 4th ch from hook, 1 tr into each ch, 3 ch, turn.

2nd row Miss first tr, 1 tr into each tr, 1 tr into next ch, 3 ch, turn. Repeat last row until work measures 10 in. [25 cm] omitting turning ch at end of last row. Fasten off.

To make up

Do not press. With $\frac{1}{2}$ in. [13 cm] seams back stitch gusset to main piece beginning and ending at rod casing.
Main section:
   Cut 1 piece *Vilene* $22\frac{1}{2} \times 9\frac{1}{2}$ in. [57 × 24 cm].
   Cut 2 pieces lining $23\frac{1}{2} \times 10\frac{1}{2}$ in. [60 × 27 cm]
Gusset:
   Cut 2 pieces *Vilene* $9\frac{1}{2} \times 3\frac{1}{2}$ in. [24 × 9 cm]
   Cut 4 pieces lining $10\frac{1}{2} \times 4\frac{1}{2}$ in. [27 × 11 cm]
Base:
   Cut 1 piece cardboard $9\frac{1}{4} \times 3\frac{1}{4}$ in. [24 × 8 cm].
Main section—Place *Vilene* centrally to wrong side of lining; turn edges of lining over *Vilene* and herringbone stitch in position. Place cardboard to wrong side at centre, to form base, and herringbone stitch across cardboard to *Vilene*. Turn in edges of remaining lining section $\frac{1}{2}$ in. [13 mm], place to wrong side and oversew.
Make up gusset sections in same manner.
Oversew gussets to main sections.
Place inside bag; catch crochet along top edge and down the gusset seams.
Insert rods of frame in position.

Sweater with knitted borders

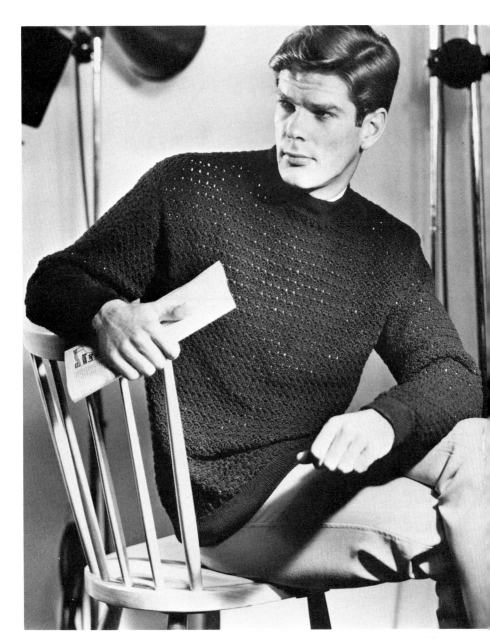

Materials

21 (22) oz Coats *Carefree Bri-Nylon* 4 ply
Milward Disc (aluminium) crochet hook
4·00 (no. 8)
Two No. 11 Milwards knitting needles
A length of narrow elastic for neck (if
desired)

Measurements

To fit 40 (42) in. [100 (106) cm] chest
Length from shoulder 25 (26) in. [64 (65)
cm]
Sleeve seam 18 (18½) in. [46 (47) cm]

Sizes

Figure in ( ) refers to larger size. Where
only one figure is given this refers to both
sizes.

Tension

4 patterns and 6 rows to 2 square in. [50
mm] over crochet.

Tension check

Before you crochet this design check your
tension by working a 3 in. [76 mm] square
in the stitch pattern (21 ch and 9 rows). If
your tension is loose use a size finer hook;
if tight use a larger hook.

Back

Commence with 129 (135) ch.

1st row (1 dc, 2 ch, 1 dc) into 3rd ch from
hook, ★ miss 2 ch, (1 dc, 2 ch, 1 dc) into
next ch; repeat from ★ to last 3 ch, miss 2
ch, 1 dc into last ch, 3 ch, turn.

2nd row 3 tr into each loop, 1 tr into turning ch, 1 ch, turn.

3rd row (1 dc, 2 ch, 1 dc) into centre tr of
each group of 3 tr, 1 dc into 3rd of 3 ch,
3 ch, turn.

The 2nd and 3rd rows form the pattern and
are repeated throughout.

Continue straight until back measures 14
(14½) in. [36 (37) cm] from beginning
finishing with 2nd row and omitting the
turning ch at end of last row.

Armhole shaping

Ss over first 11 tr (1 dc, 2 ch, 1 dc) into
next tr, pattern to last 3 groups, 1 dc into
last tr of same group as last st was worked
into, 3 ch, turn.

Continue straight in pattern until armhole
measures 9 (9½) in. [23 (24) cm], finishing
with 3rd pattern row and omitting turning ch at end of last row.

80

Shoulder shaping

1st row 1 dc into 1st loop, (2 ch, 1 dc into next loop) twice, 2 ch, 2 hlf tr into next loop, pattern to last 4 loops, 2 hlf tr into next loop, (2 ch, 1 dc into next loop) 3 times, turn.

2nd row Ss over each st and first 4 tr, 1 dc into next tr, (1 dc, 2 ch, 1 dc) into centre tr on next tr group, pattern to last 2 tr groups, 1 dc into centre tr of next group, turn.

3rd row 1 dc into first loop (2 ch, 1 dc into next loop) twice, 1 ch, 2 hlf tr into next loop, pattern to last 4 loops, 2 hlf tr into next loop, 1 ch, 1 dc into next loop, (2 ch, 1 dc into next loop) twice. Fasten off.

Front

Work as given for Back until armhole measures 7 (7½) in. [18 (19) cm], finishing with 2nd pattern row.

Neck shaping

1st row Pattern over first 13 (14) tr groups, 1 dc into centre tr of next group, 3 ch, turn.

2nd row Keeping the last loop of each st on hook, work 2 tr into first loop, yarn over and draw through all loops, pattern to end of row.

3rd row Pattern over 12 (13) tr groups, 1 dc into top of 2 tr group, 3 ch, turn.

4th row As 2nd row.

Work 3 rows.

Shoulder shaping

1st row Pattern to last 4 loops, 2 hlf tr into next loop, (2 ch, 1 dc into next loop) 3 times, turn.

2nd row Ss over each st and first 4 tr, 1 dc into next tr, (1 dc, 2 ch, 1 dc) into centre tr of next group, pattern to end of row, 3 ch, turn.

3rd row As 1st row. Fasten off.

Leaving 8 tr groups unworked in centre of front, join yarn to centre of next tr group and continue as given for first side, reversing shaping.

Sleeves

Make 57 (63) ch and work as given for Back for 3 (5) rows.

1st row 1 tr into first dc, pattern to end of row, finishing with 2 tr into turning ch, 1 ch, turn.

2nd row 1 dc into 2nd tr, pattern to end of row, 1 dc into last tr, 1 dc into turning ch, 3 ch, turn.

3rd row 2 tr into first dc, pattern to end of row, 2 tr into last dc, 1 tr into turning ch, 1 ch, turn.

4th row (1 dc, 2 ch, 1 dc) into 2nd tr, pattern to end of row, (1 dc, 2 ch, 1 dc) into last tr, 1 dc into turning ch, 3 ch, turn.

5th row 1 tr group into each loop, 1 tr into turning ch, 1 ch, turn.

6th row (1 dc, 2 ch, 1 dc) into centre tr of each group, 1 dc into 3rd of 3 ch, 3 ch, turn.

7th and 8th rows As 5th and 6th rows.

Repeat the last 8 rows 4 times more, then repeat the first 6 of these rows again. Mark this point with a coloured thread, then work 4 rows, thus finishing with same row as 6th row above, finish last row with 4 ch, turn. (These last 4 rows are set into armhole shaping and are not included in sleeve seam measurement.)

Top shaping

1st row Keeping last loop of each st on hook, work 1 tr into each of first 2 loops, yarn over and draw through all loops on hook, pattern to last 2 loops, dec over these 2 loops as at beginning of row, 1 double tr into turning ch, 2 ch, turn.

2nd row (1 dc, 2 ch, 1 dc) into 2 tr group, (1 dc, 2 ch, 1 dc) into centre tr of each group,

(1 dc, 2 ch, 1 dc) into 2 tr group, 4 ch, turn.

Repeat these 2 rows 4 times more, then the first row again. Fasten off.

Welts (back and front alike)

With No. 11 needles and right side facing pick up and knit 127 (134) sts along lower edge. Beg with a purl row continue in stocking stitch for 4 in. [10 cm]. Cast off loosely.

Cuffs

With No. 11 needles and right side facing pick up and knit 55 (60) sts along beg of sleeve and work as for Welts.

Neckband

Join right shoulder seam. With No. 11 needles and right side facing pick up and knit 117 (124) sts round neck and work as Welts for 3 in. [76 mm].

To make up

Join left shoulder seam. Sew in sleeves, sewing the last 4 rows of sleeve seams to the cast off sts at underarm. Join side and sleeve seams. Fold all borders in half and slip stitch in position, inserting elastic in neck edge if required.

Sweater

Materials

18 (19, 20, 22) oz Coats *Cadenza Courtelle* 4 ply
Milward Disc crochet hook 3·50 (no. 10)
OR
20 (21, 22, 23) oz Coats *Carefree Bri-Nylon* 4 ply
Milward Disc crochet hook 4·00 (no. 8)

Measurements

To fit 38 (40, 42, 44) in. [96 (100, 106, 112) cm] chest
Length at centre back 25 (25¾, 26½, 27¼) in. [64 (65, 67, 70) cm]
Sleeve seam 18 (18, 18½, 18½) in. [46 (46, 47, 47) cm]

Tension check

Before you crochet this design check the tension by working a 4 in. [102 mm] square in the stitch pattern (24 ch and 20 rows) using the size of hook stated. If your tension is loose use a size finer hook; if tight use a size larger hook.

Tension

11 sts and 10 rows to 2 in. [50 mm] measured over pattern.

Back

Using 3·50 (no. 10) hook for *Cadenza*, 4·00 (no. 8) hook for *Carefree* commence with 112 (116, 122, 128) ch.

1st row 1 dc into 2nd ch from hook, 1 dc into each ch, 1 ch, turn.

2nd row 1 dc into each dc, 1 ch, turn.

Repeat last row 10 times more, turning with 3 ch at end of last row.

1st row Miss first dc, * 1 dc into next dc, 1 tr into next dc; repeat from * to end, 1 ch, turn.

2nd row 1 dc into first tr, * 1 tr into next dc, 1 dc into next tr; repeat from *, working last dc into 3rd of 3 ch, 3 ch, turn.

3rd row (right side) Miss first dc, * 1 dc into next tr, 1 tr into next dc; repeat from * to end, 1 ch, turn.

Last 2 rows form pattern.

Continue in pattern until work measures 16½ in. [42 cm] or length required, ending with a 3rd pattern row and omitting turning ch at end of last row.

Armhole shaping

1st row 1 ss into each of first 6 sts, 1 dc into next tr, work in pattern to within last 6 sts, turn.

2nd row 1 ss into first dc, 1 dc into next tr, work in pattern to within last dc, turn.

Repeat last row 5 (5, 7, 7) times more, turning with 3 ch at end of last row.

Continue in pattern for 35 (37, 39, 41) rows more omitting turning ch at end of last row.

Shoulder shaping

1st and 2nd rows 1 ss into each of first 10 (8, 10, 10) sts, 3 ch, work in pattern to within last 9 (7, 9, 9) sts, turn.

3rd row 1 ss into each of first 7 (7, 4, 6) sts, 1 dc into same place as last ss, work in pattern to within last 6 (6, 3, 5) sts. Fasten off.

Front

Work as Back until 30th (32nd, 36th, 38th) row of armhole has been completed.

Neck shaping

1st row 1 dc into first tr, * 1 tr into next dc, 1 dc into next tr; repeat from * 18 (18, 18, 19) times more, turn.

2nd row 1 ss into each of first 3 sts, 3 ch, work in pattern to end.

3rd row Work in pattern to within last 2 sts, turn.

4th row 1 ss into first dc, 1 dc into next tr, work in pattern to end.

5th row Work in pattern to within last dc, turn.

Repeat last 2 rows 3 times more, turning with 3 ch at end of last row.

Next row Work in pattern, omitting turning ch at end of row, turn.

Shoulder shaping

1st row 1 ss into each of first 10 (8, 10, 10) sts, 3 ch, work in pattern to end.

2nd row Work in pattern to within last 9 (7, 9, 9) sts, turn.

3rd row 1 ss into each of first 7 (7, 4, 6) sts, 1 dc into same place as last ss, work in pattern to end omitting turning ch at end of row. Fasten off.

With wrong side facing, miss 9 (13, 15, 17) sts, attach yarn to next tr, 1 dc into same place as join and complete to correspond with first side.

Sleeves

Using 3·50 (no. 9) hook for *Cadenza*, 4·00 (no. 8) hook for *Carefree* commence with 46 (48, 50, 52) ch and work as Back for 15 rows turning with 3 ch at end of last row.

16th row 1 dc into first tr—an inc made, work in pattern to within last st, into next st work 1 dc and 1 tr—another inc made, 1 ch, turn.

17th to 19th row Work in pattern, turning with 1 ch at end of last row.

20th row Into first st work 1 dc and 1 tr, work in pattern to within last st, into next st work 1 tr and 1 dc, 3 ch, turn.

21st to 23rd row Work in pattern, turning with 3 ch at end of last row.

Repeat 16th to 23rd row twice more then 16th to 22nd row again.

Continue to inc in this manner at both ends of next and every following 3rd row until there are 81 (83, 85, 87) sts.
Continue in pattern until work measures approximately 19 (19, 19½, 19½) in. [48 (48, 49, 49) cm] or length required, ending with a 3rd pattern row and omitting turning ch at end of last row.
The last 1 in. [25 mm] is set into armhole and is not included in sleeve seam measurement.

Top shaping

1st row 1 ss into each of first 2 sts, 3 ch, work in pattern to within last st, turn.

Repeat last row 5 (5, 7, 7) times more.

Next row 1 ss into each of first 2 sts, 1 dc into next tr, work in pattern to within last 2 sts, turn.

Next row 1 ss into each of first 3 sts, 3 ch, work in pattern to within last 2 sts, turn.

Next row 1 ss into each of first 2 sts, 1 dc into next tr, work in pattern to within last 2 sts, turn.

Next row 1 ss into each of first 3 sts, 1 dc into next tr, work in pattern to within last 3 sts, turn.

Repeat last row twice more.

Next row 1 ss into each of next 5 sts, 3 ch, work in pattern to within last 4 sts, turn.

Next row 1 ss into each of next 4 sts, 1 dc into next tr, work in pattern to within last 4 sts, turn.

Next row 1 ss into each of next 5 sts, 3 ch, work in pattern to within last 4 sts. Fasten off.

Neck edging

Using a fine back stitch seam, sew shoulder seams.

1st row With right side facing and using 3·50 (no. 9) hook for *Cadenza*, 4·00 (no. 8) hook for *Carefree*, attach yarn to any shoulder seam, 1 dc into same place as join, work a row of dc evenly all round, ending with 1 ss into first dc, 1 ch, turn.

2nd row 1 dc into same place as ss, 1 dc into each dc, 1 ss into first dc, 1 ch, turn.

Repeat last row 4 times more, omitting turning ch at end of last row. Fasten off.

To make up

Do not press.
Using a fine back stitch seam sew side and neckband seams then leaving 1 in. [25 mm] free at top, sew sleeve seams then set in sleeves. Press seams lightly on the wrong side with a cool iron.

Dress

Materials

4 (5, 5) oz Coats *Cadenza Courtelle* Crepe
knits as 4 ply
Milward Disc (aluminium) crochet hook
3·50 (no. 9)
OR
4 (5, 5) oz Coats *Cadenza Courtelle* 4 ply
Milward Disc (aluminium) crochet hook
3·50 (no. 9)
OR
4 (5, 5) oz Coats *Carefree Bri-Nylon* 4 ply
Milward Disc (aluminium) crochet hook
4·00 (no. 8)
3 buttons

Measurements

To fit 18 (20, 22) in. [46 (51, 56) cm] chest
Length from shoulder 12 (14½, 16½) in.
[30 (36, 42) cm]
Sleeve seam 1 in. [25 mm] approximately

Tension

5 tr to 1 in. [25 mm].
7 rows to 3 in. [76 mm].

Tension check

Before you crochet this design check the
tension by working an approximate 3 in.

[76 mm] square in the treble (17 ch and 7
rows) using the size of hook stated. If your
tension is loose use a size finer hook; if
tight use a size larger hook.

Back

Using 3·50 (no. 9) hook for *Cadenza*, 4·00
(no. 8) hook for *Carefree* commence with
78 (83, 88) ch.

1st row 1 tr into 4th ch from hook, 1 tr into
each of next 5 (6, 7) ch, * miss 2 ch, yarn
over hook, insert hook into next ch and
draw lp up ½ in. [13 mm] (yarn over hook,
insert hook into same ch and draw lp up
as before) 3 times, yarn over and draw
through all lps on hook—a puff st made
—2 ch, a puff st into same place as last
puff st, 1 ch, miss 2 ch, 1 tr into each of
next 14 (15, 16) ch; repeat from * omitting 7 tr at end of last repeat, 3 ch, turn.

2nd row Miss first tr, * 1 tr into each st to
within next puff st, into next 2 ch sp work a
puff st 2 ch and a puff st, 1 ch; repeat from
* ending with 1 tr into each remaining st,
3 ch, turn.

2nd row forms pattern.
Work in pattern for 4 (0, 2) rows more.

Dec row Miss first tr, * 1 tr into each st to
within 2 tr before next puff st, leaving the

last lp of each on hook work 1 tr into each of next 2 tr, yarn over and draw through all lps on hook—a dec made, into next 2 ch sp work a puff st 2 ch and a puff st, 1 ch; repeat from * ending with 1 tr into each remaining st, 3 ch, turn.

Work in pattern for 2 (4, 4) rows more. Repeat last 3 (5, 5) rows 3 times more.

Next row Miss first tr, 1 tr into each st to within next puff st, * into next 2 ch sp work a puff st 2 ch and a puff st, 1 ch, 1 tr into each tr to within 2 tr before next puff st, a dec over next 2 tr; repeat from * twice more, work in pattern to end.

Work in pattern for 1 (1, 3) rows more omitting turning ch at end of last row.

Armhole shaping and back opening

1st row 1 ss into each of first 5 (6, 7) sts, 3 ch, into next 2 ch sp work a puff st 2 ch and a puff st, 1 ch, 1 tr into each tr to within next puff st, into next 2 ch sp work a puff st 2 ch and a puff st, 1 ch, 1 tr into each of next 5 (5, 6) tr, 3 ch, turn.

2nd row Work in pattern to within last 2 ch sp, a puff st into next 2 ch sp, 1 tr into 3rd of 3 ch, turn.

3rd row 1 ss into each of first 2 sts, 3 ch, 1 tr into next tr, work in pattern to end.

4th row Work in pattern to within last tr, 1 tr into next tr, 3 ch, turn.

Work in pattern for 4 (6, 6) rows more omitting turning ch at end of last row. Fasten off.

1st and 3rd sizes only

With right side facing, attach yarn to same place as last tr on 1st row of armhole shaping, 3 ch, 1 tr into each of next 4 (5) tr, work in pattern to within last 5 (7) sts, 1 tr into next tr, 3 ch, turn and complete to correspond with first side.

2nd size only

With right side facing, attach yarn to next tr at centre, 3 ch, 1 tr into each of next 4 tr, work in pattern to within last 6 sts, 1 tr into next tr, 3 ch, turn and complete to correspond with first side.

Front

Work as Back to within armhole shaping.

Armhole shaping

1st row 1 ss into each of first 5 (6, 7) sts, 3 ch, into next 2 ch sp work a puff st 2 ch and a puff st, 1 ch, work in pattern to within last 5 (6, 7) sts, 1 tr into next tr, 3 ch, turn.

2nd row A puff st into next 2 ch sp, 1 ch, work in pattern to within last 2 ch sp, a puff st into next 2 ch sp, 1 tr into 3rd of 3 ch, turn.

3rd row 1 ss into each of first 2 sts, 3 ch, work in pattern to within last puff st, 1 tr into next puff st, 3 ch, turn.

Keeping continuity of pattern work 3 (5, 5) rows more.

Neck shaping

1st row Miss first tr, 1 tr into each tr to within next puff st, a puff st into next 2 ch sp, 1 tr into next tr, turn.

2nd row 1 ss into each of first 2 sts, 3 ch, work in pattern to end.

With wrong side facing, miss 7 (8, 9) tr at centre, attach yarn to next tr, 3 ch, a puff st into next 2 ch sp and complete to correspond with first side.

Sleeves

Using 3·50 (no. 9) hook for *Cadenza*, 4·00 (no. 8) hook for *Carefree* commence with 39 (43, 47) ch.

1st row 1 tr into 4th ch from hook, 1 tr into

each of next 2 (3, 4) ch, * miss 2 ch, into next ch work a puff st 2 ch and a puff st, miss 2 ch, 1 tr into each of next 7 (8, 9) ch; repeat from * ending with miss 2 ch, 1 tr into each of next 4 (5, 6) ch, 3 ch, turn.

Work in pattern for 1 row more omitting turning ch at end of last row.

Top shaping

1st row 1 ss into each of first 4 (5, 6) sts, 3 ch, work in pattern to within last 4 (5, 6) sts, 1 tr into next tr, 3 ch, turn.

2nd row As 2nd row of Front armhole shaping.

3rd row As 3rd row of Front armhole shaping turning with 2 ch.

4th row Miss first tr, 1 tr into next tr, work in pattern to within last 2 sts, a dec over next 2 sts, 2 ch, turn.

1st size only

5th row Miss first st, 1 tr into next st, work in pattern to within last 2 tr, a dec over next 2 tr. Fasten off.

2nd and 3rd sizes only

5th row Miss first st, 1 tr into next st, work in pattern to within last 2 tr, a dec over next 2 tr, 2 ch, turn.

Repeat last row twice more omitting turning ch at end of last row. Fasten off.

To make up

Do not press.
Sew shoulder, side and sleeve seams then set in sleeves.

Neck edging

1st row Using 3·50 (no. 9) hook for *Cadenza*, 4·00 (no. 8) hook for *Carefree* commence with 1 ch, draw lp up on hook ½ in., [13 mm] 1 ch work a puff st 2 ch and a puff st, turn.

2nd row 1 ss into first st and into next sp, draw lp up as before, into same sp work a puff st 2 ch and a puff st, turn.

Repeat last row until work is long enough to fit round neck. Fasten off.
Sew neck edging in position.

Edging for back opening

1st row Using 3·50 (no. 9) hook for *Cadenza*, 4·00 (no. 8) hook for *Carefree* and with wrong side facing, attach yarn to base of back opening, work a row of dc evenly across row ends to neck edge, 1 ch, turn.

2nd row 1 dc into each dc. Fasten off.

With wrong side facing, attach yarn to neck edge of opposite side of back opening and complete to correspond with first side.

Sleeve edgings

1st row Using 3·50 (no. 9) hook for *Cadenza*, 4·00 (no. 8) hook for *Carefree* and with right side facing, attach yarn to sleeve seam, 1 dc into same place as join, work a row of dc evenly all round ending with 1 ss into first dc.

2nd row 1 dc into same place as ss, 1 dc into each dc, 1 ss into first dc. Fasten off.

Lower edging

Using 3·50 (no. 9) hook for *Cadenza*, 4·00 (no. 8) hook for *Carefree* and with right side facing, attach yarn to any side seam and complete to correspond with sleeve edging.

To complete

Sew buttons in position using row ends as buttonholes.
Press all seams lightly on the wrong side with a cool iron.

Dress

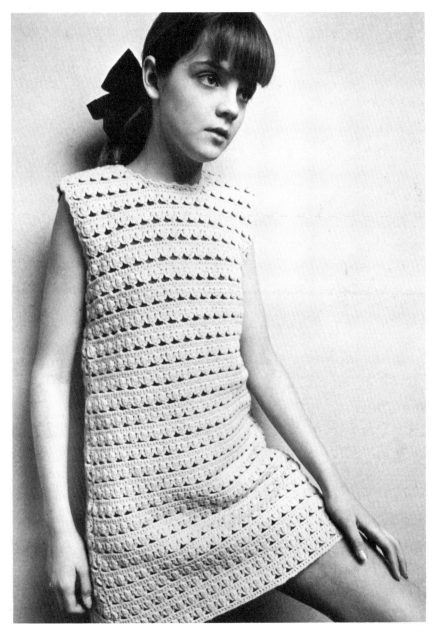

Materials

12 (13, 14) oz Coats *Carefree Bri-Nylon*
Baby Quick Knit
Milward Disc (aluminium) crochet hook
5·00 (no. 6)

Measurements

To fit 28 to 29 (30, 32) in. [71 to 73 (75, 80)
cm] chest
Actual measurement $31\frac{1}{2}$ (33, $34\frac{1}{2}$) in. [79
(84, 88) cm]
Length from shoulder $25\frac{3}{4}$ ($27\frac{1}{2}$, $30\frac{1}{4}$) in.
[65 (70, 77) cm]

Tension check

Before you crochet this design check the
tension by working an approximate 6 in.

[152 mm] square in the stitch pattern (34 ch
and 25 rows) using the size of hook stated.
If your tension is loose use a size finer hook;
if tight use a size larger hook.

Tension

4 patterns to 3 in. [76 mm].
3 rows of clusters to $2\frac{1}{2}$ in. [64 mm].

Front

Make 8 ch and leave aside for Armhole
shaping.

Left shoulder

Commence with 22 ch.

1st row 1 dc into 2nd ch from hook, * 3 ch,
miss 1 ch, leaving the last loop of each on
hook work 3 tr into next ch, yarn over and

draw through all loops on hook—a 3 tr cluster made, 3 ch, miss 1 ch, 1 dc into next ch; repeat from * ending with 4 ch, turn.

2nd row (right side) 1 dc into first cluster, * 3 ch, 1 dc into next cluster; repeat from * ending with 1 ch, 1 tr into next dc, 1 ch, turn.

3rd row 1 dc into first tr, 1 dc into next sp, * 1 dc into next dc, 3 dc into next sp; repeat from * ending with 1 dc into next dc, 1 dc into next sp, 1 dc into 3rd of 4 ch, 1 ch, turn.

4th row 1 dc into each dc, 1 ch, turn.

5th row 1 dc into first dc, * 3 ch, miss 1 dc, a 3 tr cluster into next dc, 3 ch, miss 1 dc, 1 dc into next dc; repeat from * ending with 3 ch, turn.

Neck shaping

1st row 1 tr into first dc, 2 ch, 1 dc into next cluster, * 3 ch, 1 dc into next cluster; repeat from * ending with 1 ch, 1 tr into next dc, 1 ch, turn.

2nd row 1 dc into first tr, 1 dc into next sp, * 1 dc into next dc, 3 dc into next sp; repeat from * ending with 1 dc into next dc, 2 dc into next sp, 1 dc into next tr, 2 dc into 3rd of 3 ch, 1 ch, turn.

3rd row 2 dc into first dc, 1 dc into each dc, 1 ch, turn.

4th row 1 dc into first dc, * 3 ch, miss 1 dc, a 3 tr cluster into next dc, 3 ch, miss 1 dc, 1 dc into next dc; repeat from * to end. Fasten off.

Right shoulder

Work as Left shoulder for 5 rows ending last row with 4 ch, turn.

Neck shaping

1st row 1 dc into first cluster, * 3 ch, 1 dc into next cluster; repeat from * ending with 2 ch, 2 tr into next dc, 1 ch, turn.

2nd row 2 dc into first tr, 1 dc into next tr, 2

dc into next sp, * 1 dc into next dc, 3 dc into next sp; repeat from * ending with 1 dc into next dc, 1 dc into next sp, 1 dc into 3rd of 4 ch, 1 ch, turn.

3rd row 1 dc into each dc to within last dc, 2 dc into last dc, 1 ch, turn.

4th row 1 dc into first dc, * 3 ch, miss 1 dc, a 3 tr cluster into next dc, 3 ch, miss 1 dc, 1 dc into next dc; repeat from * 5 times more, 4 ch, turn.

5th row 1 dc into first cluster, (3 ch, 1 dc into next cluster) 5 times, 2 ch, 1 tr into next dc, 17 (21, 25) ch, 1 tr into last dc worked on Left side, 2 ch, (1 dc into next cluster, 3 ch) 5 times, 1 dc into next cluster, 1 ch, 1 tr into next dc, 1 ch, turn.

6th row 1 dc into first tr, 1 dc into next sp, (1 dc into next dc, 3 dc into next sp) 5 times, 1 dc into next dc, 2 dc into next sp, 1 dc into next tr, 1 dc into each of next 17 (21, 25) ch, 1 dc into next tr, 2 dc into next sp, (1 dc into next dc, 3 dc into next sp) 5 times, 1 dc into next dc, 1 dc into next sp, 1 dc into 3rd of 4 ch, 1 ch, turn.

7th row 1 dc into each dc, 1 ch, turn.

8th row 1 dc into first dc, * 3 ch, miss 1 dc, a 3 tr cluster into next dc, 3 ch, miss 1 dc, 1 dc into next dc; repeat from * ending with 4 ch, turn.

9th row 1 dc into first cluster, * 3 ch, 1 dc into next cluster; repeat from * ending with 1 ch, 1 tr into next dc, 1 ch, turn.

10th row 1 dc into first tr, 1 dc into next sp, * 1 dc into next dc, 3 dc into next sp; repeat from * ending with 1 dc into next dc, 1 dc into next sp, 1 dc into 3rd of 4 ch, 1 ch, turn.

Last 4 rows form pattern.
Work in pattern for 8 (8, 12) rows more turning with 9 ch at end of last row.

Armhole shaping

1st row 1 dc into 2nd ch from hook, 1 dc into each of next 7 ch, 1 dc into each dc, attach length of ch already worked to same place as last dc, 1 dc into each of next 8 ch, 1 ch, turn.

Work in pattern for 14 (14, 18) rows more.

Side shaping

1st row 2 dc into first tr, 1 dc into next sp, work in pattern to within last st, 2 dc into last st, 1 ch, turn.

2nd row 2 dc into first dc, 1 dc into each dc to within last dc, 2 dc into last dc, 3 ch, turn.

3rd row 1 tr into first dc, 3 ch, miss 1 dc, 1 dc into next dc, work in pattern to within last 2 dc, 3 ch, a 2 tr cluster into last dc, 1 ch, turn.

4th row 1 dc into first cluster, 3 ch, work in pattern ending with 3 ch, 1 dc into next tr, 1 ch, turn.

5th row 1 dc into first dc, work in pattern ending with 1 dc into last dc, 1 ch, turn.

6th row 1 dc into each dc, 3 ch, turn.

Repeat last 4 rows once more, then 3rd and 4th rows again.

13th row 2 dc into first dc, work in pattern to within last dc, 2 dc into last dc, 1 ch, turn.

14th row As 2nd row of Side shaping ending with 1 ch, turn.

15th to 24th row Work in pattern.

Repeat 1st to 24th row once more, then 1st to 18th row again.
Work in pattern for 8 (16, 20) rows more, or length required, ending with a 7th pattern row and omitting turning ch at end of last row. Fasten off.

Back

Make 8 ch and leave aside for Armhole shaping.

Left shoulder

Commence with 22 ch and work as Left
94

shoulder of Front for 1 row ending with 3 ch, turn.

Neck shaping

Work as Neck shaping on Left shoulder of Front.

Right shoulder

Commence with 22 ch and work as Right shoulder of Front for 1 row.

Neck shaping

Work as Neck shaping on Right shoulder of Front for 10 rows.
Work in pattern for 12 (12, 16) rows more turning with 9 ch at end of last row.

Armhole shaping

As armhole shaping of Front.
Complete as Front.

To make up

Do not press. Sew shoulder and side seams.

Neck edging

1st row With right side facing, attach yarn to any shoulder seam and work a row of dc neatly all round having a multiple of 4 dc, 1 ss into first dc.

2nd row * Into next dc work 1 dc 3 ch and 1 dc, miss 1 dc, 1 dc into next dc, miss 1 dc; repeat from * ending with 1 ss into first dc. Fasten off.

Armhole edging

With right side facing, attach yarn to underarm seam and complete as Neck edging.

To complete

Press all seams lightly on the wrong side with a cool iron.

Cardigan

Materials

6 (7, 8) oz Coats *Carefree Bri-Nylon* 4 ply
One Milward Disc crochet hook 4·00
(no. 8)
OR
5 (6, 6) oz Coats *Cadenza Courtelle* 4 ply
One Milward Disc crochet hook 3·50 (no.
9) 5 (6, 7) buttons

Measurements

To fit 22 (24, 26) in. [56 (61, 65) cm] chest
Length from shoulder 11¼ (13¾, 15½) in.
[26 (30, 39) cm] approximately
Sleeve seam 9 (11, 11) in. [23 (28, 28) cm]
approximately

Tension check

Before you crochet this design check the
tension by working a 4 in. [102 mm] square
in the stitch pattern (24 ch and 14 rows)
using the size of hook stated. If your tension is loose, use a size finer hook; if tight,
use a size larger hook.

Tension

6 sts to 1 in. [25 mm]
6 rows to 1¾ in. [44 mm]

Back

Using 4·00 (no. 8) hook for *Carefree* 3·50
(no. 9) hook for *Cadenza* commence with
74 (80, 86) ch.

1st row 1 dc into 2nd ch from hook, * 1 ch,
miss 1 ch, 1 dc into next ch; repeat from *
ending with 2 ch, turn.

2nd row 1 tr into first sp, * 1 ch leaving the
last loop of each on hook work 1 tr into
same sp as last tr and 1 tr into next sp, yarn
over and draw through all loops on hook
—a joint tr made; repeat from * ending
with 1 ch, a joint tr over same sp and next
dc, 2 ch, turn.

3rd row 1 tr into first sp, * 1 ch, a joint tr
over same sp and next sp; repeat from *
ending with 1 ch, a joint tr over same sp and
next tr, 1 ch, turn.

4th row 1 dc into first joint tr, * 1 ch, 1 dc
into next joint tr; repeat from * working
last dc into last tr, 2 ch, turn.

2nd to 4th row forms pattern.

Work in pattern for 17 (23, 29) rows more,
omitting turning ch at end of last row.

Armhole shaping

1st row 1 ss into each of first 6 sts, 1 dc into
next joint tr, 1 ch, work in pattern to within
last 3 sps, 2 ch, turn.

Work in pattern for 13 (16, 16) rows more,
omitting turning ch at end of last row.

Shoulder shaping

1st row 1 ss into each of first 8 (10, 10) sts, 2
ch, 1 hlf tr into next sp, 1 ch, work in pattern to within last 4 (5, 5) sps, 1 ch, yarn
over hook, insert hook into same sp as last
tr and draw loop through, yarn over hook,

insert hook into next sp and draw loop through, yarn over and draw through all loops on hook (a joint hlf tr made), turn.

2nd row 1 ss into each of first 6 sts, 1 dc into next joint tr, 1 ch, work in pattern to within last 3 sps. Fasten off.

Front

First side

Using 4·00 (no. 8) hook for *Carefree*, 3·50 (no. 9) hook for *Cadenza* commence with 36 (38, 42) ch and work as Back for 21 (27, 33) rows, omitting turning ch at end of last row on 2nd and 3rd sizes only.

Armhole shaping

1st size only

1st row Work in pattern to within last 3 sps, 2 ch, turn.

2nd and 3rd sizes only

1st row 1 ss into each of first 6 sts, 1 dc into next st, work in pattern to end of row.

All sizes

Work in pattern for 8 (11, 11) rows more.

Neck shaping

1st row Work in pattern to within last 3 (3, 4) sps, turn.

2nd row 1 ss into each of first 2 sts, 2 ch, 1 tr into next sp, 1 ch, work in pattern to end of row.

3rd row Work in pattern to within last sp, 1 ch, a joint tr over same sp and last tr, 1 ch, turn.

4th and 5th rows Work in pattern.

Shoulder shaping

1st row Work in pattern to within last 4 (5, 5) sps, 1 ch, a joint hlf tr over same sp and next sp turn.

2nd row 1 ss into each of first 6 sts, 1 dc into next joint tr work in pattern to end of row omitting turning ch at end. Fasten off.

Second side

Work to correspond with First side.

Sleeves

Using 4·00 (no. 8) hook for *Carefree*, 3·50 (no. 9) hook for *Cadenza* commence with 32 (36, 36) ch and work as Back for 2 rows, turning with 3 ch at end of last row.

1st increase row A joint tr over first joint tr and next sp, 1 ch, work in pattern ending with 1 tr into same place as last tr, 1 ch, turn.

2nd increase row 1 dc into first tr, 1 ch, 1 dc into next joint tr, work in pattern ending with 1 ch, 1 dc into 3rd of 3 ch, 2 ch, turn.

Work in pattern for 4 rows more, ending last row with 3 ch, turn.
Repeat last 6 rows 3 (4, 4) times more, then first 4 rows again omitting turning ch at end of last row.

Top shaping

1st row 1 ss into each of first 6 sts, 1 dc into next joint tr, work in pattern to within last 3 sps, 3 ch, turn.

2nd row A joint tr over first 2 sps, work in pattern to within last sp, 1 ch, a joint tr over same sp and next sp, 1 tr into next dc, 2 ch, turn.

3rd row Miss first joint tr, 1 tr into next sp, 1 ch, work in pattern working last joint tr over last sp and 3rd of 3 ch, 2 ch, turn.

4th row Miss first joint tr, 1 dc into next joint tr, work in pattern to within last sp, 1 hlf tr into last tr, 2 ch, turn.

5th row 1 tr into first sp, work in pattern working last joint tr over last sp and 2nd of 2 ch, 2 ch, turn.

6th row Miss first sp, 1 tr into next sp, work in pattern to within last sp, a joint tr over same sp and last tr, 2 ch, turn.

7th row Miss first joint tr, 1 dc into next joint tr, work in pattern to within last sp, 1 hlf tr into last tr, 3 ch, turn.

8th row A joint tr over first 2 sps, work in pattern to within last dc, 1 tr into 2nd of 2 ch, 3 ch, turn.

9th row A joint tr over first 2 sps, work in pattern to within last joint tr, 1 tr into 3rd of 3 ch, 2 ch, turn.

10th row Miss first joint tr, 1 dc into next joint tr, work in pattern to within last joint tr, 1 hlf tr into 3rd of 3 ch, 2 ch, turn.

11th row Miss first sp, 1 hlf tr into next sp, 1 ch, work in pattern to within last sp, 1 ch, a joint hlf tr over same sp and 2nd of 2 ch. Fasten off.

To make up

Do not press. Using a flat seam sew shoulder, side and sleeve seams, and set in sleeves.

Jacket edging

1st row With right side facing and using 4·00 (no. 8) hook for *Carefree*, 3·50 (no. 9) hook for *Cadenza* attach yarn to left side seam, 1 dc into same place as join, work a row of dc evenly all round working 3 dc into each corner st and having a multiple of 3 dc, 1 ss into first dc.

2nd row 1 dc into same place as ss, (1 dc into each dc to within centre dc at next corner, 3 dc into next dc) twice, 1 dc into each of next 4 (4, 6) dc, (insert hook into next dc and draw yarn through) twice, yarn over and draw through all loops on hook —a joint dc made, 1 dc into each of next 2 dc, a joint dc over next 2 dc, 1 dc into each dc working 2 joint dc on opposite side of

neck to correspond and having 3 dc into centre dc at each corner, 1 ss into first dc.

Mark the position of 5 (6, 7) buttonholes evenly spaced on Right front.

3rd row 1 dc into same place as ss, 1 dc into each dc, to within centre dc at next corner, 3 dc into next dc, 1 dc into each dc to within centre dc at next corner working buttonholes to correspond with markings—to make a buttonhole work 3 ch, miss 3 dc, 1 dc into next dc—3 dc into centre dc at corner, 1 dc into each of next 4 dc, a joint dc over next 2 sts, 1 dc into next dc, a joint dc over next 2 sts, 1 dc into each dc working 2 joint dc on opposite side of neck to correspond and having 3 dc into centre dc at each corner, 1 ss into first dc.

4th row 1 dc into same place as ss, 1 dc into each dc—working 3 dc into centre dc at each corner, 3 dc into each buttonhole and having a joint dc over each joint dc as before, 1 ss into first dc.

5th row 1 dc into same place as ss, * 3 ch, 1 dc into last dc worked, 1 dc into each of next 3 sts; repeat from * omitting 1 dc at end of last repeat, 1 ss into first dc. Fasten off.

Sleeve edgings

1st row With right side facing and using 4·00 (no. 8) hook for *Carefree*, 3·50 (no. 9) hook for *Cadenza*, attach yarn to seam, 1 dc into same place as join, work a row of dc, evenly all round having a multiple of 3 dc, 1 ss into first dc.

2nd to 4th row 1 dc into same place as ss, 1 dc into each dc, 1 ss into first dc.

5th row As 5th row of Jacket edging.

To complete

Sew on buttons to correspond with buttonholes.

Cardigan

Materials

6 (7, 8) oz Coats *Carefree Bri-Nylon* 4 ply
Milward Disc (aluminium) crochet hook
4·00 (no. 8) [3·50 (no. 9), 4·00 (no. 8)]
OR
5 (6, 7) oz Coats *Cadenza Courtelle* 4 ply
Milward Disc (aluminium) crochet hook
3·50 (no. 9) [3·00 (no. 11), 3·50 (no. 9)]
6 buttons

Measurements

To fit 22 (24, 26) in. [56 (61, 65) cm] chest
Length at centre back 16¼ (18¼, 19¼) in.
[41 (46, 49) cm] including edgings
Sleeve seam 10 (13, 13) in. [25 (33, 33) cm]

Pattern tension

First 5 rows 2 (1¾, 2) in. [50 (44, 50) mm]
using 4·00 (no. 8) (3·50 (no. 9), 4·00 (no. 8))
hook for *Carefree*, 3·50 (no. 9) (3·00 (no.
11), 3·50 (no. 9)) hook for *Cadenza*.
1 pattern 1½ (1¼, 1½) in. [38 (32, 38) mm]
using 4·00 (no. 8) (3·50 (no. 9), 4·00 (no. 8))
hook for *Carefree*, 3·50 (no. 9) (3·00 (no.
11), 3·50 (no. 9)) hook for *Cadenza*.

Tension check

Before you crochet this design check the
tension by working a square of approximately 4 (3½, 4) in. [102 (89, 102) mm] in
the stitch pattern (26 ch and 13 rows), using
the size of hook stated. If your tension is
loose use a size finer hook; if tight use a
size larger hook.

Back

Using 4·00 (no. 8) [3·50 (no. 9), 4·00 (no.
8)] hook for *Carefree*, 3·50 (no. 9) [3·00
(no. 11), 3·50 (no. 9)] hook for *Cadenza*,
commence with 66 (82, 82) ch.

1st row 1 dc into 2nd ch from hook, 2 ch,
miss 3 ch, leaving the last lp of each on hook
work 3 tr into next ch, yarn over and draw
through all lps on hook—a 3 tr cluster
made, 2 ch, a 3 tr cl into same ch, ★ 2 ch,
miss 3 ch, 1 dc into next ch, 2 ch, miss 3 ch,
into next ch work a 3 tr cl 2 ch and a 3 tr cl
—a shell made; repeat from ★ omitting 2
ch and a shell at end of last repeat, 3 ch,
turn.

2nd row (right side) A 3 tr cl into first dc, ★ 2
ch, 1 dc into sp of next shell, 2 ch, a shell
into next dc; repeat from ★ omitting a shell
at end of last repeat, a 3 tr cl and 1 tr into
last dc, 1 ch, turn.

3rd row 1 dc into first tr, ★ 2 ch, a shell into
next dc, 2 ch, 1 dc into sp of next shell;
repeat from ★ ending with 2 ch, 1 dc into
3rd of 3 ch, 3 ch, turn.

2nd and 3rd rows form pattern.

Continue in pattern for 22 (24, 26) rows
more, or length required, ending with a 3rd
pattern row and omitting turning ch at end
of last row.

Armhole shaping

1st row 1 ss into each of first 4 sts, 1 dc into
next sp, 2 ch, work in pattern to within last
shell, 1 dc into sp of next shell, turn.

Repeat last row once more, turning with 3 ch.

Continue in pattern for 10 (12, 12) rows more omitting turning ch at end of last row.

Shoulder shaping

1st row As 1st row of armhole shaping.

Repeat last row 2 (3, 3) times more. Fasten off.

Left front

Using 4·00 (no. 8) [3·50 (no. 9), 4·00 (no. 8)] hook for *Carefree*, 3·50 (no. 9) [3·00 (no. 11), 3·50 (no. 9)] hook for *Cadenza*, commence with 34 (42, 42) ch and work as Back to armhole shaping.

Armhole shaping

1st row 1 ss into each of first 4 sts, 1 dc into next sp, 2 ch, work in pattern to end.

2nd row Work in pattern to within last shell, 1 dc into centre of next shell, 3 ch, turn.

Continue in pattern for 6 (8, 8) rows more.

Neck shaping

1st row Work in pattern to within last shell, 1 dc into centre of last shell, turn.

2nd row 1 ss into each of first 4 sts, 1 dc into next sp, 2 ch, work in pattern to end.

3rd row Work in pattern to within last shell, 1 dc into centre of last shell, 2 ch, 1 tr into last dc, 3 ch, turn.

4th row A 3 tr cl into first dc, 2 ch, work in pattern to end omitting turning ch.

Shoulder shaping

1st row 1 ss into each of first 4 sts, 1 dc into next sp, 2 ch, work in pattern ending with 1 dc into last cl, 3 ch, turn.

1st size only

2nd row A 3 tr cl into first dc, 2 ch, 1 dc into centre of last shell. Fasten off.

2nd and 3rd sizes only

2nd row Work in pattern to within last shell, 1 dc into sp of last shell, turn.

3rd row 1 ss into each of first 4 sts, 1 dc into next sp, 2 ch, a shell into next dc, 2 ch, 1 dc into next cl, 3 ch, turn.

4th row A 3 tr cl into first dc, 2 ch, 1 dc into centre of next shell. Fasten off.

Right front

Using 4·00 (no. 8) (3·50 (no. 9), 4·00 (no. 8)) hook for *Carefree*, 3·50 (no. 9) (3·00 (no. 11), 3·50 (no. 9)) hook for *Cadenza*, work to correspond with Left front.

Sleeves

Using 4·00 (no. 8) [3·50 (no. 9), 4·00 (no. 8)] hook for *Carefree*, 3·50 (no. 9) [3·00 (no. 11), 3·50 (no. 9)] hook for *Cadenza*, commence with 42 (50, 50) ch and work as Back for 7 (9, 9) rows.

1st increase row A shell into first dc, work in pattern to within last dc, a shell and 1 tr into last dc, 3 ch, turn.

2nd increase row 1 tr into first cl, 2 ch, 1 dc into next sp, work in pattern to within last shell, 2 ch, 1 dc into sp of next shell, 2 ch, 1 tr into next cl, 1 tr into 3rd of 3 ch, 1 ch, turn.

3rd increase row 1 dc into first tr, 2 ch, work in pattern ending with 1 dc into 3rd of 3 ch, 3 ch, turn.

1st size only

Continue in pattern for 18 rows more, or length required, ending with a 3rd pattern row and omitting turning ch at end of last row.

2nd and 3rd sizes only

Continue in pattern for 10 rows more then repeat 1st to 3rd increase rows once more. Continue in pattern for 8 rows more, or length required, ending with a 3rd pattern row and omitting turning ch at end of last row.

Top shaping   All sizes

1st row 1 ss into each of first 4 sts, 1 dc into next sp, 2 ch, work in pattern to within last shell, 1 dc into sp of next shell, turn.

Repeat last row 3 (4, 4) times more. Fasten off.

Sleeve edgings

1st row Using 4·00 (no. 8) [3·50 (no. 9), 4·00 (no. 8)] hook for *Carefree*, 3·50 (no. 9) [3·00 (no. 11), 3·50 (no. 9)] hook for *Cadenza* and with right side facing, attach yarn to same place as first dc on 1st row and work a row of dc evenly across foundation ch, 1 ch, turn.

2nd row 1 dc into each dc, 1 ch, turn.

Repeat last row 3 times more omitting turning ch at end of last row. Fasten off.

To make up

Do not press. Using a flat seam, sew side, shoulder and sleeve seams then set in sleeves.

Neck, front and lower edging

1st row Using 4·00 (no. 8) [3·50 (no. 9), 4·00 (no. 8)] hook for *Carefree*, 3·50 (no. 9) [3·00 (no. 11), 3·50 (no. 9)] hook for *Cadenza* and with right side facing, attach yarn to left shoulder seam, work a row of dc evenly all round working 3 dc into each corner at neck and lower edge, ending with 1 ss into first dc, 1 ch, turn.

2nd row 1 dc into each dc, working 3 dc into centre dc at each corner, 1 ss into first dc, 1 ch, turn.

3rd row Before commencing mark the position of 6 buttonholes evenly across right front, 1 dc into each dc working 3 dc into each corner making buttonholes to correspond with markings—to make a buttonhole 3 ch, miss 3 dc, 1 dc into next dc —1 ss into first dc, 1 ch, turn.

4th row 1 dc into each dc, working 3 dc into centre dc at each corner and 3 dc into each buttonhole, 1 ss into first dc.

5th row As 2nd row omitting turning ch. Fasten off.

To complete

Sew on buttons to correspond with buttonholes.

Dress

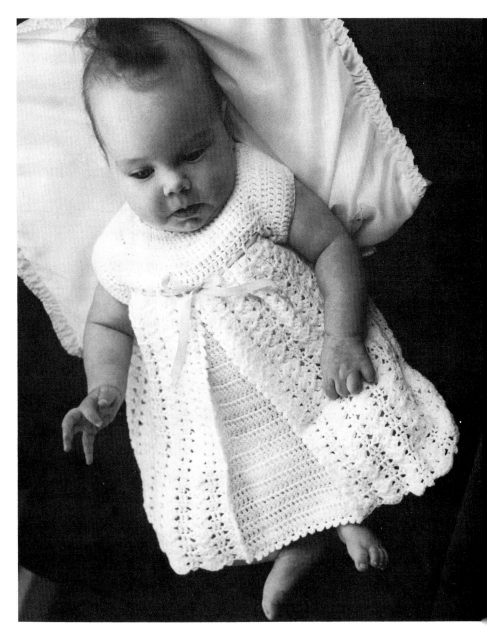

Materials

5 oz Coats *Carefree Bri-Nylon* 3 ply
Milward Disc (aluminium) crochet hook
3·50 (no. 9)
2 small buttons
1 yd [91 cm] nylon ribbon ⅜ in. [10 mm]
wide

Measurements

To fit 18 to 20 in. [46 to 50 cm] chest
Length at centre back 14 in. [36 cm]

Tension

5 tr and 3 rows to 1 in. [25 mm]

Tension check

Before you crochet this design check your
tension by working a 3 in. [76 mm] square
in tr pattern (17 ch and 9 rows). If your
tension is loose use a size finer hook; if
tight use a larger hook.

104

Yoke

Commence with 69 ch (fairly tight).

1st row 1 tr into 4th ch from hook, 1 tr into
each of next 12 ch, 3 tr into next ch, 1 tr into
each of next 5 ch, 3 tr into next ch, 1 tr into
each of next 25 ch, 3 tr into next ch, 1 tr
into each of next 5 ch, 3 tr into next ch, 1 tr
into each of next 14 ch, 3 ch, turn.

2nd row Miss first tr, 1 tr into each of next
14 tr, 3 tr into next tr, 1 tr into each of next
7 tr, 3 tr into next tr, 1 tr into each of next
27 tr, 3 tr into next tr, 1 tr into each of next
7 tr, 3 tr into next tr, 1 tr into each of next
14 tr, 1 tr into 3rd of 3 ch, 3 ch, turn.

3rd row Miss first tr, 1 tr into each of next
15 tr, 3 tr into next tr, 1 tr into each of next
9 tr, 3 tr into next tr, 1 tr into each of next
29 tr, 3 tr into next tr, 1 tr into each of next
9 tr, 3 tr into next tr, 1 tr into each of next
15 tr, 1 tr into 3rd of 3 ch, 3 ch, turn.

Continue in this manner for 3 rows more
working 3 tr into centre tr of each 3 tr group
having extra tr between each group and
omitting turning ch at end of last row.
Fasten off.

Skirt front

1st row Miss first 3 tr group, attach yarn to
3rd tr of next 3 tr group, 5 ch, miss next tr,
(1 tr into next tr, 2 ch, miss next tr) 8 times,
1 tr into next tr, 16 ch, 1 ss into top of last
tr, (2 ch, miss next tr, 1 tr into next tr) 9
times, 3 ch, turn.

2nd row (right side) 2 tr into first sp, (1 tr
into next tr, 3 tr into next sp) 7 times, 1 tr
into next tr, 2 tr into next sp, 1 tr into next
tr, 1 tr into each of next 16 ch (pleat), 1 tr
into same tr before pleat, 2 tr into next sp,
(1 tr into next tr, 3 tr into next sp) 7 times, 1
tr into next tr, 2 tr into next sp, 1 tr into 3rd
of 5 ch, 3 ch, turn.

3rd row Miss first 2 tr, 3 tr 1 ch and 3 tr into
next tr (shell made), ★ miss 2 tr, 2 tr into

next tr, miss 2 tr, shell into next tr; repeat from * 3 times more, miss 2 tr, 2 tr into next tr, miss 2 tr, 3 tr into next tr (half shell made), miss 2 tr, 1 tr into each of next 16 tr of pleat, 3 tr into next tr (half shell made), miss 2 tr, 2 tr into next tr, miss 2 tr, shell into next tr; repeat from * to * 4 times more, 1 tr into 3rd of 3 ch, 3 ch, turn.

4th row Shell into first 1 ch sp (shell over shell), * miss 3 tr of shell, 1 tr into each of next 2 tr, shell over next shell; repeat from * 3 times more, miss 3 tr of shell, 1 tr into each of next 2 tr, miss 2 tr, half shell into next tr, 1 tr into each tr of pleat, half shell into next tr, miss 2 tr, 1 tr into each of next 2 tr, shell over next shell; repeat from * to * 4 times more, 1 tr into 3rd of 3 ch, 3 ch, turn.

5th row Work in pattern until first half shell is completed, 1 tr into each of next 4 tr, 2 tr into next tr, 1 tr into each tr to within last 5 tr of pleat, 2 tr into next tr, 1 tr into each of next 4 tr and continue in pattern to end of row, 3 ch, turn.

6th and 7th rows As 4th row.

8th row As 5th row.

9th row As 4th row.

Repeat last 4 rows until work measures $13\frac{1}{2}$ in. [34 cm] or length required, omitting turning ch at end of last repeat. Fasten off.

Skirt back

Overlap last 3 sts to first 3 sts on last row of yoke and sew in position.

1st row With wrong side facing, miss 19 tr, attach yarn to next tr, 5 ch, miss 1 tr, 1 tr into next tr, (2 ch, miss 1 tr, 1 tr into next tr) 17 times, 3 ch, turn.

2nd row 2 tr into first sp, * 1 tr into next tr, 3 tr into next sp; repeat from * working last tr into 3rd of 5 ch, 3 ch, turn.

3rd row Miss first 2 tr, * shell into next tr, miss 2 tr, 2 tr into next tr, miss 2 tr; repeat

from * ending with shell into next tr, 1 tr into 3rd of 3 ch, 3 ch, turn.

Continue in pattern until work measures $13\frac{1}{2}$ in. [34 cm] or length required, omitting turning ch at end of last row. Fasten off.

Leaving first 5 rows of skirt open for armhole, sew side seams. Sew pleat in position to top of first row of skirt.

Sleeves

1st row With right side facing, attach yarn to side seam, 3 ch, 2 tr into each of next 5 row ends, 1 tr into same place as next st on yoke, 1 tr into each of next 19 tr, 1 tr into same place as next st on yoke, 2 tr into each of next 5 row ends, 1 ss into 3rd of 3 ch (42 sts).

2nd row 3 ch, 1 tr into each tr, 1 ss into 3rd of 3 ch.

3rd row 1 ch, 1 dc into same place as ss, 1 dc into each tr, 1 ss into first dc.

4th row 1 ch, 1 dc into same place as ss, * miss 1 dc, 1 dc into each of next 2 dc; repeat from * omitting 1 dc at end of last repeat, 1 ss into first dc.

5th row 1 dc into each dc, 1 ss into first dc. Fasten off.

Lower edging

With right side facing, attach yarn into any shell, 3 ch, 5 tr into same place as join, * miss next 3 tr of shell, 1 tr into next st, 3 ch, 1 dc into 3rd ch from hook (picot made), 1 tr into next st, 6 tr over next shell; repeat from * to pleat ending with half shell over half shell, 1 tr into each tr of pleat, half shell over half shell; repeat from * to * omitting 6 tr at end of last repeat, 1 ss into 3rd of 3 ch. Fasten off.

Neck edging

With right side facing, attach yarn to foundation ch at neck edge, into same place as join work 1 dc 3 ch and 1 dc, * miss 1 ch, into next ch work 1 dc 3 ch and 1 dc; repeat from * to end. Fasten off.

Pleat edging

With right side facing, attach yarn to tr at top of pleat, into same place as join work 1 dc 3 ch and 1 dc, over each tr to lower edge work 1 dc 3 ch and 1 dc, * into next tr work 1 dc 3 ch and 1 dc, miss 1 tr; repeat from * along lower edge and complete other edge of pleat to correspond. Fasten off.

To make up

Cut one piece of ribbon 8 in. [20 cm] long and thread through spaces on 1st row of Back and secure.
Cut remaining ribbon in half and thread through spaces 6n 1st row of Front, secure and tie in a bow.
Sew 2 buttons in position on yoke having top button on 1st row of yoke and second button on 4th row. (Using space between 2nd and 3rd stitch on opposite side as buttonhole.)

Bonnet and mitts

Materials

2 oz Coats *Carefree Bri-Nylon* Baby Quick Knit
One 4·00 (no. 8) Milward Disc crochet hook
Bonnet 1 yd [91 cm] 1 in. [25 mm] wide ribbon
Mitts 1 yd [91 cm] of narrow ribbon

Measurements

Bonnet All round face, 12 in. [31 mm]
Mitts Width, 2¾ in. [70 mm]

Tension

5 dc to 1 in. [25 mm] in width.

Bonnet

Crown

Commence with 4 ch, join with ss to form ring.

1st round Work 8 dc into ring.

Working into back loop of st on every round for remainder of Crown and mark-

ing beginning of each round with a pin, shape Crown as follows:

2nd round 2 dc into each dc.

3rd round ★ 1 dc into next dc, 2 dc into next dc; repeat from ★ to end of round.

4th round ★ 1 dc into each of next 2 dc, 2 dc into next dc; repeat from ★ to end of round.

5th round ★ 1 dc into each of next 3 dc, 2 dc into next dc; repeat from ★ to end of round.

Continue inc in this manner until the round '★ 1 dc into each of next 7 dc, 2 dc into next dc; repeat from ★ to end of round' has been worked (72 dc).
Work 3 rounds without shaping.

Next round 1 dc into each of next 8 dc, ★ miss 1 dc, 1 dc into each of next 7 dc; repeat from ★ to end of round (64 dc).

Do not break off yarn.
Proceed in rows for Main part of bonnet as follows:

1st row Working through both loops of dc, work 1 dc into each of next 52 dc, turn.

2nd row Working into back loop of dc, work 1 ch, miss first dc, 1 dc into next dc, miss 1 dc, ★ 4 tr into next dc, miss 1 dc, 1 dc into next dc, miss 1 dc; repeat from ★ 11 times, 1 dc into next dc, turn.

3rd row Working into remaining loop of dc on 1st row, work 1 ch, miss first dc, 1 dc into each remaining 51 dc, turn.

Working through both loops of st for remainder of Main part continue as follows:

4th row 3 ch, miss first dc, 1 tr into each remaining dc, turn.

5th row 4 ch, miss first tr, ★ 1 Cl into next tr, 1 ch, miss 1 tr, 1 dc into next tr, 1 ch, miss 1 tr; repeat from ★ 11 times, 1 Cl into next tr, 1 ch, miss 1 tr, 1 tr into 3rd of 3 ch, turn.

6th row 3 ch, 1 tr into first 1 ch sp, ★ 2 tr into next 1 ch sp, repeat from ★ to end, turn.

7th row 1 ch, miss first tr, 1 dc into each of next 1 ch sp; repeat from * to end, turn.

Repeat rows 4 to 7 once.

Do not break off yarn.
Work Edging as follows:

With right side facing, work a row of dc down first side of Main part, across lower edge of Crown, up second side of Main part, then working through both loops of dc on 7th row of Main part, work 1 ch, miss first dc, 1 dc into next dc, miss next dc, * 4 tr into next dc, miss 1 dc, 1 dc into next dc, miss 1 dc; repeat from * 11 times, 1 dc into next dc. Fasten off.

To make up

Press very lightly on wrong side using a cool iron.
Cut ribbon into two lengths and attach to each side of Bonnet.

Mitts

Commence with 24 ch, join with ss to form ring.

1st round Work 1 dc into each ch, 1 ss into first dc (24 dc).

2nd round 3 ch, miss first dc, 1 tr into each of remaining 23 dc, 1 ss into 3rd of 3 ch.

3rd round 1 dc into same place as ss, (1 ch, miss 1 tr, 1 Cl into next tr, 1 ch, miss 1 tr, 1 dc into next tr) 5 times, 1 ch, miss 1 tr, 1 Cl into next tr, 1 ch, 1 ss into first dc.

4th round 3 ch, 1 tr into first 1 ch sp, * 2 tr into next 1 ch sp; repeat from * to end of round, 1 ss into 3rd of 3 ch.

5th round 1 dc into same place as ss, 1 dc into each remaining tr, 1 ss into first dc.

6th round 3 ch, miss first dc, 1 tr into each of remaining 23 dc, 1 ss into 3rd of 3 ch.

7th round 1 dc into same place as ss, 1 dc into each of remaining 23 tr, 1 ss into first dc.

Working into back loop of st on every round for remainder of Mitt and marking beginning of each round with a pin, continue as follows:

8th round (2 dc into next dc, 1 dc into each of next 11 dc) twice.

9th round 1 dc into each dc.

10th round (2 dc into next dc, 1 dc into each of next 12 dc) twice (28 dc).

11th to 14th round As 9th.

15th round (1 dc into next dc, miss 1 dc, 1 dc into each of next 10 dc, miss 1 dc, 1 dc into next dc) twice.

16th round As 9th.

17th round (1 dc into next dc, miss 1 dc, 1 dc into each of next 8 dc, miss 1 dc, 1 dc into next dc) twice.

18th round As 9th.

19th round (1 dc into next dc, miss 1 dc, 1 dc into each of next 6 dc, miss 1 dc, 1 dc into next dc) twice. Fasten off.

Edging

With right side facing, attach yarn to first of commencing ch. Work 1 dc into first ch, (miss 1 ch, 4 tr into next ch, miss 1 ch, 1 dc into next ch) 5 times, miss 1 ch, 4 tr into next ch, 1 ss into first dc. Fasten off.

To make up

Press very lightly on wrong side using a cool iron.
Using a flat seam, join seam.
Press seam.
Thread ribbon through last row of tr on cuff.

Materials

2 oz Coats *Carefree Bri-Nylon* Baby Quick Knit
One 3·50 (no. 9) Milward Disc crochet hook
Bonnet 1 yd [91 cm] 1 in. [25 mm] wide ribbon
Mitts 1 yd [91 cm] of narrow ribbon

Measurements

Bonnet All round face, 12¼ in. [31 cm]
Mitts Width all round, 5 in. [127 mm]

Tension

5½ dc to 1 in. [25 mm] in width
6 rows dc to 1 in. [25 mm] in height
2 Cr 2 Tr to 1⅛ in. [29 mm] in width

Bonnet

Main part

Commence with 70 ch.

1st row Miss first ch, 1 dc into each remaining ch, 1 ch, turn.

2nd row 3 ch, miss 3 dc, * 1 dc into next dc, 3 ch, miss 2 dc; repeat from * ending with 1 dc into turning ch, 3 ch, turn (23 sp).

Proceed in pattern as follows:

1st row * Cr 2 Tr; repeat from * ending with 1 tr into turning ch, 1 ch, turn.

2nd row * 3 ch, 1 dc into centre of Cr 2 Tr; repeat from * ending with 3 ch, 1 dc into top of turning ch, 3 ch, turn.

These 2 rows form the pattern.

Continue in pattern until work measures approximately 4 in. [10 cm] from beginning, finishing at end of a 2nd row of pattern, omitting 3 ch at end of last row. Fasten off.

Back piece

With right side facing and leaving nine 3 ch sp free, attach yarn to next dc, 3 ch, (Cr 2 Tr) 4 times, 1 tr into next dc, 1 ch, turn.

Continue in pattern on these sts until work measures approximately 6 in. [15 cm] from beginning of Back piece, finishing at end of a 1st row, omitting 1 ch at end of last row. Fasten off.

To make up

Using a flat seam, join Back piece to Main part.
With right side facing, attach yarn to first of commencing ch, into same ch work 1 dc, 1 dc into each remaining ch across front of Main part, 1 ch, turn.

Next row Miss first dc, 1 dc into each remaining dc, 1 ch, turn.

Repeat last row 5 times, omitting 1 ch at end of last row. Fasten off.

Work 2 rows of dc along lower edge of Bonnet. Fasten off.

To complete make-up

Fold 6 rows of dc to right side, neatly stitching ends to Main part.

Press seams.
Cut ribbon into two lengths and attach to each side of Bonnet as in photograph.

Mitts

Commence with 28 ch.

1st row Miss first ch, 1 dc into each remaining ch, 1 ch, turn.

2nd row 3 ch, miss 3 dc, * 1 dc into next dc, 3 ch, miss 2 dc, repeat from * ending with 1 dc into turning ch, 3 ch, turn (9 sp).

Work 4 rows of pattern as on Bonnet, finishing with 1 ch at end of last row.

Next row (2 dc into 3 ch sp, 1 dc into next dc) 8 times, 2 dc into next 3 ch sp, 1 dc into turning ch, 1 ch, turn (28 dc).

Next row Miss first dc, 1 dc into each remaining dc, 1 ch, turn.

Repeat last row until work measures 4 in. [10 cm] from beginning, finishing with right side facing for next row.

Shape as follows:

1st row Miss first dc, 1 dc into next dc, * miss 1 dc, 1 dc into each of next 8 dc, miss 1 dc, * 1 dc into each of next 4 dc; repeat from * to * once, 1 dc into each of next 2 dc, 1 ch, turn.

2nd row Miss first dc, 1 dc into each remaining dc, 1 ch, turn.

3rd row Miss first dc, 1 dc into next dc, * miss 1 dc, 1 dc into each of next 6 dc, miss 1 dc, * 1 dc into each of next 4 dc; repeat from * to * once, 1 dc into each of next 2 dc, 1 ch, turn.

4th row As 2nd.

5th row Miss first dc, 1 dc into next dc, * miss 1 dc, 1 dc into each of next 4 dc; repeat from * twice, miss 1 dc, 1 dc into each of next 2 dc, 1 ch, turn.

6th row Miss first dc, 1 dc into each remaining dc. Fasten off.

To make up

Block and press very lightly on wrong side using a cool iron.
Using a flat stitch, join seam.
Press seam.
Thread ribbon through last row of holes on cuff.

111

Jacket

Materials

3 (4, 5) oz Coats *Carefree Bri-Nylon* 3 ply
Milward Disc crochet hook 3·50 (no. 9)
3 small buttons

Measurements

To fit 20 (22, 24) in. [51 (56, 61) cm] chest
Length at centre back $9\frac{1}{2}$ ($11\frac{1}{2}$, 13) in. [24
(29, 33) cm] approximately
Sleeve seam $4\frac{1}{2}$ (5, 6) in. [114 (127, 152)
mm] approximately

Tension

3 sps and first 3 rows to 1 square in. [25
square mm].
If your crochet is loose use a size finer hook,
if tight use a size larger hook.

Yoke 1st and 2nd sizes only

Commence with 68 ch.

1st row 1 tr into 6th ch from hook, (1 ch,
miss 1 ch, 1 tr into next ch) 5 times, 1 ch,
into next ch work 1 tr 1 ch and 1 tr—a V st
made—1 ch, 1 tr into next ch, (1 ch, miss 1
ch, 1 tr into next ch) twice, 1 ch, a V st into
next ch, 1 ch, 1 tr into next ch, (1 ch, miss 1
ch, 1 tr into next ch) 12 times, 1 ch, a V st
into next ch, 1 ch, 1 tr into next ch, (1 ch,

miss 1 ch, 1 tr into next ch) twice, 1 ch, a V st into next ch, 1 ch, 1 tr into next ch, (1 ch, miss 1 ch, 1 tr into next ch) 6 times, 4 ch, turn.

2nd row (right side) Miss first tr, a pc st into next tr, (1 ch, 1 tr into next tr, 1 ch, a pc st into next tr) 3 times, 1 ch, a V st into next sp, (1 ch, a pc st into next tr, 1 ch, 1 tr into next tr) twice, 1 ch, a pc st into next tr, 1 ch, a V st into next sp, (1 ch, a pc st into next tr, 1 ch, 1 tr into next tr) 7 times, 1 ch, a pc st into next tr, 1 ch, a V st into next sp, (1 ch, a pc st into next tr, 1 ch, 1 tr into next tr) twice, 1 ch, a pc st into next tr, 1 ch, a V st into next sp, (1 ch, a pc st into next tr 1 ch, 1 tr into next tr) 3 times, 1 ch, a pc st into next tr, 1 ch, miss 1 ch, 1 tr into next ch, 4 ch, turn.

3rd row Miss first tr, (1 tr into next pc st 1 ch, 1 tr into next tr, 1 ch) 4 times, a V st into next sp, (1 ch, 1 tr into next tr, 1 ch, 1 tr into next pc st) 3 times, 1 ch, 1 tr into next tr 1 ch, a V st into next sp, (1 ch, 1 tr into next tr, 1 ch, 1 tr into next pc st) 8 times, 1 ch, 1 tr into next tr, 1 ch, a V st into next sp, (1 ch, 1 tr into next tr, 1 ch, 1 tr into next pc st) 3 times, 1 ch, 1 tr into next tr 1 ch, a V st into next sp, (1 ch, 1 tr into next tr, 1 ch, 1 tr into next pc st) 4 times, 1 ch, 1 tr into 3rd of 4 ch, 4 ch, turn.

2nd and 3rd rows form Yoke pattern.
Work in pattern for 4 (6) rows more, having one pc st more on each Front and 2 pc sts more on each of Back and Sleeve sections and ending last row with 3 ch, turn.

Yoke 3rd size only

Commence with 80 ch.

1st row 1 tr into 6th ch from hook, (1 ch, miss 1 ch, 1 tr into next ch) 6 times, 1 ch, into next ch work 1 tr 1 ch and 1 tr—a V st made—, 1 ch, 1 tr into next ch, (1 ch, miss 1 ch, 1 tr into next ch) 3 times, 1 ch, a V st into next ch, 1 ch, 1 tr into next ch, (1 ch, miss 1 ch, 1 tr into next ch) 14 times, 1 ch, a

114

V st into next ch, 1 ch, 1 tr into next ch, (1 ch, miss 1 ch, 1 tr into next ch) 3 times, 1 ch, a V st into next ch, 1 ch, 1 tr into next ch, (1 ch, miss 1 ch, 1 tr into next ch) 7 times, 4 ch, turn.

2nd row (right side) Miss first tr, a pc st into next tr, (1 ch, 1 tr into next tr, 1 ch, a pc st into next tr) 3 times, 1 ch, 1 tr into next tr, 1 ch, a V st into next sp, (1 ch, 1 tr into next tr, 1 ch, a pc st into next tr) 3 times, 1 ch, a V st into next sp, (1 ch, a pc st into next tr, 1 ch, 1 tr into next tr) 8 times, 1 ch, a pc st into next tr, 1 ch, a V st into next sp, (1 ch, a pc st into next tr, 1 ch, 1 tr into next tr) 3 times, 1 ch, a V st into next sp, (1 ch, 1 tr into next tr, 1 ch, a pc st into next tr) 4 times, 1 ch, miss 1 ch, 1 tr into next ch, 4 ch, turn.

3rd row Miss first tr, (1 tr into next pc st, 1 ch, 1 tr into next tr, 1 ch) 4 times, 1 tr into next tr, 1 ch, a V st into next sp, (1 ch, 1 tr into next tr) twice, (1 ch, 1 tr into next pc st, 1 ch, 1 tr into next tr) 3 times, 1 ch, a V st into next sp, (1 ch, 1 tr into next tr, 1 ch, 1 tr into next pc st) 9 times, 1 ch, a tr into next tr, 1 ch, a V st into next sp, (1 ch, 1 tr into next tr, 1 ch, 1 tr into next pc st) 3 times, (1 ch, 1 tr into next tr) twice, 1 ch, a V st into next sp, (1 ch, 1 tr into next tr) twice, (1 ch, 1 tr into next pc st, 1 ch, 1 tr into next tr) 3 times, 1 ch, 1 tr into next pc st, 1 ch, 1 tr into 3rd of 4 ch, 4 ch, turn.

2nd and 3rd rows form Yoke pattern.
Work in pattern for 6 rows more, having one pc st more on each Front and 2 pc sts more on each of Back and Sleeve sections and ending last row with 3 ch, turn.

Skirt all sizes

1st row Miss first tr, * 2 tr into next sp, 1 tr into next tr; repeat from * 12 (14, 15) times more, 2 tr into next sp, leaving the last lp of each on hook work 1 tr into next tr miss 15 (19, 20) tr and 1 tr into next tr, yarn over and draw through all lps on hook—a joint tr made—, * 2 tr into next sp, 1 tr into next tr; repeat from * 26 (30, 32) times more,

2 tr into next sp, a joint tr as before, ** 2 tr into next sp, 1 tr into next tr; repeat from ** working last tr into 3rd of 4 ch, 5 ch, turn.

2nd row Miss first 3 tr, * 1 tr into next st, 2 ch, miss 2 tr; repeat from * ending with 1 tr into 3rd of 3 ch, 3 ch, turn.

3rd row Miss first tr, * 2 tr into next sp, 1 tr into next tr; repeat from * working last tr into 3rd of 5 ch 5 ch, turn.

2nd and 3rd rows form skirt pattern. Work in pattern for 17 (21, 25) rows more, or length required ending with a 2nd pattern row.

Last row Miss first tr, * 2 tr into next sp, 1 tr into next tr, 3 ch, 1 dc into last tr; repeat from * to within last sp, 2 tr into sp, 1 tr into 3rd of 5 ch. Fasten off.

Sleeves 1st and 2nd sizes only

1st row With right side facing, attach yarn to joint tr at underarm, 4 ch, a pc st into same place as tr of joint tr, * 1 ch, 1 tr into next tr, 1 ch, a pc st into next tr; repeat from * working last pc st into same place as tr of joint tr, 1 ch, 1 ss into 3rd of 4 ch, 4 ch, turn.

2nd row 1 tr into next pc st, * 1 ch, 1 tr into next tr, 1 ch, 1 tr into next pc st; repeat from * ending with 1 ch, 1 ss into 3rd of 4 ch, 4 ch, turn.

3rd row A pc st into next tr, * 1 ch, 1 tr into next tr, 1 ch, a pc st into next tr; repeat from * ending with 1 ch, 1 ss into 3rd of 4 ch, 4 ch, turn.

Repeat last 2 rows 5 (6) times more, omitting turning ch at end of last row.

Sleeves 3rd size only

1st row With right side facing, attach yarn to joint tr at underarm, 4 ch, a pc st over next bar of same joint tr, 1 ch, 1 tr into base

of same tr, (1 ch, a pc st into next tr, 1 ch, 1 tr into next tr) 10 times, 1 ch, a pc st into same place as tr of joint tr, 1 ch, 1 ss into 3rd of 4 ch, 4 ch, turn.

2nd and 3rd rows As 2nd and 3rd rows of 1st size.

Repeat last 2 rows 7 times more, omitting turning ch at end of last row.

Sleeve edging all sizes

1st row 1 dc into same place as ss, * 1 dc into each of next 2 sps, 1 dc into next tr; repeat from * omitting 1 dc at end of last repeat, 1 ss into first dc.

2nd row 1 dc into same place as ss, 1 dc into each dc, 1 ss into first dc.

3rd row 1 dc into same place as ss, * 3 ch, 1 dc into last dc, 1 dc into each of next 3 dc; repeat from * omitting 1 dc at end of last repeat; 1 ss into first dc. Fasten off.

Front and neck edging

1st row With right side facing attach yarn to lower edge of right front, 2 dc over same row-end, 2 dc over each row-end across front, 5 dc into corner sp, 2 dc into each 1 ch sp and 1 dc into same place as each V st round neck, 5 dc into next corner sp, 2 dc over each row-end across front, 1 ch, turn.

2nd row 1 dc into each dc, working 3 dc into centre dc at each corner, making 3 buttonholes evenly spaced across right yoke—to make buttonhole 2 ch, miss 2 dc, 1 dc into next dc—ending with 1 ch, turn.

3rd row 1 dc into each dc, working 2 dc into each buttonhole and 3 dc into centre dc at each corner. Fasten off.

To complete

Do not press. Sew buttons to edging of left yoke to correspond with buttonholes.

Dress and coat

Materials

5 oz Coats *Baby Orlon*
Milward Disc (aluminium) crochet hook
3·50 (no. 9)
If your crochet is loose, use a size finer
hook; if tight, use a size larger hook
5 small buttons
2 yd [183 mm] ribbon $\frac{3}{8}$ in. [10 mm] wide

Measurements

Dress To fit chest 18 to 20 in. [46 to 51 cm].
Length from shoulder 16 in. [41 cm].
Coat To fit chest 18 to 20 in. [46 to 51 cm].
Length from shoulder 16 in. [41 cm].
Length of sleeve $4\frac{3}{4}$ in. [12 cm].

Tension

5 tr to 1 in. [25 mm] and first 5 rows to
2 in. [50 mm].

Dress

Yoke

Commence with 69 ch.

1st row (right side of work) 1 tr into 4th ch
from hook, 1 tr into each of next 12 ch, 3 tr
into next ch, 1 tr into each of next 5 ch, 3 tr
into next ch, 1 tr into each of next 25 ch, 3
tr into next ch, 1 tr into each of next 5 ch, 3
tr into next ch, 1 tr into each of next 14 ch,
3 ch, turn.

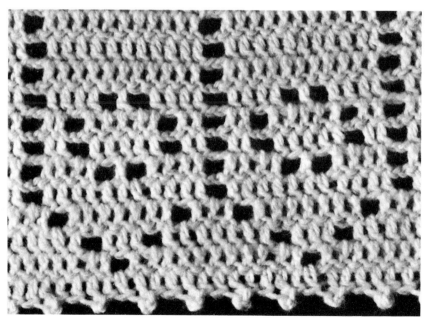

2nd row Miss first tr, 1 tr into each of next 14 tr, 3 tr into next tr, 1 tr into each of next 7 tr, 3 tr into next tr, 1 tr into each of next 27 tr, 3 tr into next tr, 1 tr into each of next 7 tr, 3 tr into next tr, 1 tr into each of next 14 tr, 1 tr into top of turning ch, 3 ch, turn.

Continue in this manner for 3 rows more working 3 tr into centre tr of each 3 tr group having extra tr between each group and omitting turning ch at end of last row. Fasten off.

Skirt front

1st row With wrong side facing, miss last 3 tr group worked on last row, attach yarn to centre tr of next 3 tr group, 4 ch, (miss next tr, 1 tr into next tr, 1 ch) 17 times, miss next tr, 1 tr into next tr, 3 ch, turn.

2nd row 3 tr into first sp, ★ 1 tr into next tr, 3 tr into next sp; repeat from ★ ending with 1 tr into 3rd of 4 ch, 3 ch, turn. (73 sts).

3rd row Miss first tr, 1 tr into each of next 5 tr, (2 ch, miss next tr, 1 tr into each of next 11 tr) 5 times, 2 ch, miss next tr, 1 tr into each of next 5 tr, 1 tr into 3rd of 3 ch, 3 ch, turn.

4th row Miss first tr, 1 tr into each of next 5 tr, (2 ch, 1 tr into each of next 11 tr) 5 times, 2 ch, 1 tr into each of next 5 tr, 1 tr into 3rd of 3 ch, 3 ch, turn.

Repeat last row 21 times more, omitting turning ch at end of last row. Fasten off. Overlap last 3 sts to first 3 sts of last row and sew in position.

Skirt back

1st row With wrong side facing, miss next 15 tr, attach yarn to next tr, 4 ch, (miss next tr, 1 tr into next tr, 1 ch) 17 times, miss next tr, 1 tr into next tr, 3 ch, turn and complete as Skirt front.

Leaving first 6 rows of skirt open for armhole, sew side seams.

Skirt edging

1st row With right side of Back facing, attach yarn to top of tr before last 2 ch sp, 5 ch, miss first sp, ★ 1 tr into each of next 4 tr, 2 ch, 1 tr into side seam, 2 ch, miss next tr, 1 tr into each of next 4 tr, (2 ch, miss next sp, 1 tr into each of next 4 tr, 2 ch, miss next tr, 1 tr into next tr, 2 ch, miss next tr, 1 tr into each of next 4 tr) 5 times, 2 ch, miss next sp; repeat from ★ once more omitting 1 tr and 2 ch at end of repeat, 1 ss into 3rd of 5 ch, 3 ch, turn.

2nd row 1 tr into next tr, ★ 2 ch, miss next tr, (1 tr into next tr, 1 tr into next sp) twice, 1 tr into next tr, 2 ch, miss next tr, 1 tr into each of next 2 tr, 2 ch, miss next sp, 1 tr into each of next 2 tr; repeat from ★ omitting 2 tr at end of last repeat, 1 ss into 3rd of 3 ch, 5 ch, turn.

3rd row Miss first sp, ★ 1 tr into each of next 2 tr, 2 ch, miss next sp, 1 tr into each of next 5 tr, 2 ch, miss next sp, 1 tr into each of next 2 tr, 2 ch, miss next sp; repeat from ★ omitting 1 tr and 2 ch at end of last repeat, 1 ss into 3rd of 5 ch, 3 ch, turn.

4th row 1 tr into next tr, ★ 1 tr into next sp, 1 tr into next tr, (2 ch, miss next tr, 1 tr into next tr) twice, 1 tr into next sp, 1 tr into each of next 2 tr, 2 ch, miss next sp, 1 tr into each of next 2 tr; repeat from ★ omitting 2 tr at end of last repeat, 1 ss into 3rd of 3 ch, 5 ch, turn.

5th row Miss first sp, ★ 1 tr into each of next 4 tr, 1 tr into next sp, 1 tr into next tr, 1 tr into next sp, 1 tr into each of next 4 tr, 2 ch, miss next sp; repeat from ★ omitting 1 tr and 2 ch at end of last repeat, 1 ss into 3rd of 5 ch, 5 ch, turn.

6th row Miss next tr, ★ 1 tr into each of next 7 tr, 2 ch, miss next tr, 1 tr into next tr, 1 tr into next sp, 1 tr into next tr, 2 ch, miss next tr; repeat from ★ omitting 1 tr and 2 ch at end of last repeat, 1 ss into 3rd of 5 ch, 3 ch, turn.

7th row 1 tr into each of next 2 tr, * 1 tr into next tr, 1 tr into next tr, 2 ch, miss next tr, 1 tr into each of next 3 tr, 2 ch, miss next tr, 1 tr into next tr, 1 tr into next sp, 1 tr into each of next 3 tr; repeat from * omitting 3 tr at end of last repeat, 1 ss into 3rd of 3 ch, 3 ch, turn.

8th row 1 tr into each of next 2 tr, * 1 tr into next sp, 1 tr into next tr, 2 ch, miss next tr, 1 tr into next tr, 1 tr into next sp, 1 tr into each of next 7 tr; repeat from * omitting 3 tr at end of last repeat, 1 ss into 3rd of 3 ch, 3 ch, turn.

9th row 1 tr into each of next 2 tr, 3 ch, 1 ss into top of last tr worked (picot made), * 1 tr into each of next 3 tr, picot, 1 tr into next tr, 1 tr into next sp, 1 tr into next tr, picot, (1 tr into each of next 3 tr, picot) twice; repeat from * omitting 3 tr and picot at end of last repeat, 1 ss into 3rd of 3 ch. Fasten off.

Sleeves (both alike)

1st row With right side facing attach yarn to side seam, 3 ch, 1 tr into first row-end, 2 tr into each of next 5 row-ends, 1 tr into each free tr, 2 tr into each of next 6 row-ends, 1 ss into 3rd of 3 ch (39 st).

2nd row 3 ch, 1 tr into each tr, 1 ss into 3rd of 3 ch.

3rd row 1 dc into each tr, 1 ss into first dc.

4th row 1 dc into each dc, 1 ss into first dc. Fasten off.

Neck edging

1st row With right side facing, attach yarn to commencing ch at left side of back opening, 3 ch, 1 tr into each of next 3 ch, * picot, miss 2 ch, 1 tr into next ch; repeat from * to within last 3 ch, 1 tr into each of next 3 ch. Fasten off.

Coat
Yoke

Commence with 73 ch.

1st row 1 tr into 4th ch from hook, 1 tr into each of next 14 ch, 3 tr into next ch, 1 tr into each of next 5 ch, 3 tr into next ch, 1 tr into each of next 25 ch, 3 tr into next ch, 1 tr into each of next 5 ch, 3 tr into next ch, 1 tr into each of next 16 ch, 3 ch, turn.

2nd row Miss first tr, 1 tr into each of next 16 tr, 3 tr into next tr, 1 tr into each of next 7 tr, 3 tr into next tr, 1 tr into each of next 27 tr, 3 tr into next tr, 1 tr into each of next 7 tr, 3 tr into next tr, 1 tr into each of next 16 tr, 1 tr into top of turning ch, 3 ch, turn.

Continue in this manner for 3 rows more working 3 tr into centre tr of each 3 tr group having extra tr between each group.

Right skirt front

1st row Miss first tr, 1 tr into each of next 3 tr, (1 ch, miss next tr, 1 tr into next tr) 9 times, 3 ch, turn.

2nd row 3 tr into first sp, * 1 tr into next tr, 3 tr into next sp; repeat from * 7 times more, 1 tr into each of next 3 tr, 1 tr into 3rd of 3 ch, 3 ch, turn. (40 sts).

3rd row Miss first tr, 1 tr into each of next 8 tr, (2 ch, miss next tr, 1 tr into each of next 11 tr) twice, 2 ch, miss next tr, 1 tr into each of next 5 tr, 1 tr into 3rd of 3 ch, 3 ch, turn.

4th row Miss first tr, 1 tr into each of next 5 tr, (2 ch, 1 tr into each of next 11 tr) twice, 2 ch, 1 tr into each of next 8 tr, 1 tr into 3rd of 3 ch, 3 ch, turn.

5th row Miss first tr, 1 tr into each of next 8 tr, (2 ch, 1 tr into each of next 11 tr) twice, 2 ch, 1 tr into each of next 5 tr, 1 tr into 3rd of 3 ch, 3 ch, turn.

Repeat last 2 rows 10 times more, omitting turning ch at end of last row. Fasten off.

Skirt back

1st row With wrong side facing, miss next 15 tr, attach yarn to next tr, 4 ch, (miss next tr, 1 tr into next tr, 1 ch) 17 times, miss next tr, 1 tr into next tr, 3 ch, turn.

2nd to 25th row Repeat 2nd to 25th row of Skirt front of dress.

Left skirt front

1st row With wrong side facing, miss next 15 tr, attach yarn to next tr, 4 ch, (miss next tr, 1 tr into next tr, 1 ch) 8 times, miss next tr, 1 tr into each of next 3 tr, 1 tr into 3rd of 3 ch, 3 ch, turn.

2nd row Miss first tr, 1 tr into each of next 3 tr, * 3 tr into next sp, 1 tr into next tr; repeat from * 8 times more working last tr into 3rd of 4 ch, 3 ch, turn (40 sts).

3rd row Miss first tr, 1 tr into each of next 5 tr, (2 ch, miss next tr, 1 tr into each of next 11 tr) twice, 2 ch, miss next tr, 1 tr into each of next 8 tr, 1 tr into 3rd of 3 ch, 3 ch, turn.

4th row Miss first tr, 1 tr into each of next 8 tr, (2 ch, 1 tr into each of next 11 tr) twice, 2 ch, 1 tr into each of next 5 tr, 1 tr into 3rd of 3 ch, 3 ch, turn.

5th row Miss first tr, 1 tr into each of next 5 tr, (2 ch, 1 tr into each of next 11 tr) twice, 2 ch, 1 tr into each of next 8 tr, 1 tr into 3rd of 3 ch, 3 ch, turn.

Repeat last 2 rows 10 times more. Do not fasten off.
Leaving first 6 rows of skirt open for armhole, sew side seams.

Skirt edging

1st row Pick up yarn at Left skirt front, miss first tr, 1 tr into each of next 3 tr, * 2 ch, miss next tr, 1 tr into each of next 4 tr, 2 ch, miss next sp, 1 tr into each of next 4 tr, 2 ch, miss next tr, 1 tr into next tr; repeat from * ending with 1 tr into each of last 2 tr and into 3rd of 3 ch, 3 ch, turn.

2nd row Miss first tr, 1 tr into each of next 3 tr, * 1 tr into next sp, 1 tr into next tr, 2 ch, miss next tr, 1 tr into each of next 2 tr, 2 ch, miss next sp, 1 tr into each of next 2 tr, 2 ch, miss next tr, 1 tr into next tr, 1 tr into next

sp, 1 tr into next tr; repeat from * ending with 1 tr into each of next 2 tr, 1 tr into 3rd of 3 ch, 3 ch, turn.

3rd row Miss first tr, * 1 tr into each of next 5 tr, 2 ch, miss next sp, (1 tr into each of next 2 tr, 2 ch, miss next sp) twice; repeat from * ending with 1 tr into each of next 5 tr, 1 tr into 3rd of 3 ch, 3 ch, turn.

4th row Miss first tr, 1 tr into each of next 3 tr, * 2 ch, miss next tr, 1 tr into next tr, 1 tr into next sp, 1 tr into each of next 2 tr, 2 ch, miss next sp, 1 tr into each of next 2 tr, 1 tr into next sp, 1 tr into next tr, 2 ch, miss next tr, 1 tr into next tr; repeat from * ending with 1 tr into each of next 2 tr, 1 tr into 3rd of 3 ch, 3 ch, turn.

5th row Miss first tr, 1 tr into each of next 3 tr, * 1 tr into next sp, 1 tr into each of next 4 tr, 2 ch, miss next sp, 1 tr into each of next 4 tr, 1 tr into next sp, 1 tr into next tr; repeat from * ending with 1 tr into each of next 2 tr, 1 tr into 3rd of 3 ch, 3 ch, turn.

6th row Miss first tr, 1 tr into each of next 6 tr, * 2 ch, miss next tr, 1 tr into next tr, 1 tr into next sp, 1 tr into next tr, 2 ch, miss next tr, 1 tr into next 7 tr; repeat from * working last tr into 3rd of 3 ch, 3 ch, turn.

7th row Miss first tr, 1 tr into each of next 4 tr, * 2 ch, miss next tr, 1 tr into next tr, 1 tr into next sp, 1 tr into each of next 3 tr, 1 tr into next sp, 1 tr into next tr, 2 ch, miss next tr, 1 tr into each of next 3 tr; repeat from * ending with 1 tr into next tr, 1 tr into 3rd of 3 ch, 3 ch, turn.

8th row Miss first tr, 1 tr into each of next 2 tr, * 2 ch, miss next tr, 1 tr into next tr, 1 tr into next sp, 1 tr into each of next 7 tr, 1 tr into next sp, 1 tr into next tr; repeat from * ending with 2 ch, miss next tr, 1 tr into each of next 2 tr, 1 tr into 3rd of 3 ch, 6 ch, turn.

9th row 1 ss into 4th ch from hook, * 1 tr into each of next 2 tr, 1 tr into next sp, picot, (1 tr into each of next 3 tr, picot) 3 times; repeat from * ending with 1 tr into each of next 2 tr, 1 tr into next sp, picot,

1 tr into each of next 2 tr, 1 tr into 3rd of 3 ch, picot. Fasten off.

Neck edging

1st row With right side of work facing, attach yarn to commencing ch at neck edge of Right front, 3 ch, 1 tr into each of next 3 ch, * picot, miss 2 ch, 1 tr into next ch; repeat from * to within last 4 ch, 1 tr into each of next 4 ch. Fasten off.

Right sleeve

1st row With right side of work facing, attach yarn to 6th row-end of Right front, 2 ch, 1 tr into 6th row-end of Back, 2 tr into each of next 5 row-ends, 1 tr into each tr, 2 tr into each of next 5 row-ends, 1 ss into first tr, (36 sts), 3 ch, turn.

2nd row 1 tr into each of next 5 tr, (2 ch, miss next tr, 1 tr into each of next 11 tr) twice, 2 ch, miss next tr, 1 tr into each of next 5 tr, 1 ss into 3rd of 3 ch, 3 ch, turn.

3rd row 1 tr into each of next 5 tr, (2 ch, miss next sp, 1 tr into each of next 11 tr) twice, 2 ch, miss next sp, 1 tr into each of next 5 tr, 1 ss into 3rd of 3 ch, 3 ch, turn. Repeat last row twice more, ending 5th row with 5 ch, turn.

6th row Miss next tr, * 1 tr into each of next 4 tr, 2 ch, miss next sp, 1 tr into each of next 4 tr, 2 ch, miss next tr, 1 tr into next tr, 2 ch, miss next tr; repeat from * omitting 1 tr and 2 ch at end of last repeat, 1 ss into 3rd of 5 ch, 3 ch, turn.

7th row * 1 tr into next sp, 1 tr into next tr, 2 ch, miss next tr, 1 tr into each of next 2 tr, 2 ch, miss next sp, 1 tr into each of next 2 tr, 2 ch, miss next tr, 1 tr into next tr, 1 tr into next sp, 1 tr into next tr; repeat from * omitting 1 tr at end of last repeat, 1 ss into 3rd of 3 ch, 3 ch, turn.

8th row * (1 tr into each of next 2 tr, 2 ch, miss next sp) 3 times, 1 tr into each of next 3 tr; repeat from * omitting 1 tr at end of last repeat, 1 ss into 3rd of 3 ch, 5 ch, turn.

9th row Miss next tr, * 1 tr into next tr, 1 tr into next sp, 1 tr into each of next 2 tr, 2 ch, miss next sp, 1 tr into each of next 2 tr, 1 tr into next sp, 1 tr into next tr, 2 ch, miss next tr, 1 tr into next tr, 2 ch, miss next tr; repeat from * omitting 1 tr and 2 ch at end of last repeat, 1 ss into 3rd of 5 ch, 3 ch, turn.

10th row 1 tr into first sp, * 1 tr into each of next 4 tr, 2 ch, miss next sp, 1 tr into each of next 4 tr, 1 tr into next sp, 1 tr into next tr, 1 tr into next sp; repeat from * omitting 2 tr at end of last repeat, 1 ss into 3rd of 3 ch, 3 ch, turn.

11th row 1 tr into each of next 3 tr, * 2 ch, miss next tr, 1 tr into next tr, 1 tr into next sp, 1 tr into next tr, 2 ch, miss next tr, 1 tr into each of next 7 tr; repeat from * omitting 4 tr at end of last repeat, 1 ss into 3rd of 3 ch, 3 ch, turn.

12th row 1 tr into next tr, * 2 ch, miss next tr, 1 tr into next tr, 1 tr into next sp, 1 tr into each of next 3 tr, 1 tr into next sp, 1 tr into next tr, 2 ch, miss next tr, 1 tr into each of next 3 tr; repeat from * omitting 2 tr at end of last repeat, 1 ss into 3rd of 3 ch, 1 ss into next tr, 4 ch, turn.

13th row Miss next st, * 1 tr into next tr, 1 tr into next sp, 1 tr into each of next 7 tr, 1 tr into next sp, 1 tr into next tr, 1 ch, miss next tr; repeat from * omitting 1 tr and 1 ch at end of last repeat, 1 ss into 3rd of 4 ch.

14th and 15th rows 1 dc into each st, 1 ss into first dc. Fasten off.

Left sleeve

With right side facing, attach yarn to 6th row-end of Back, 2 ch, 1 tr into 6th row-end of Left front and complete as Right sleeve.

To make up

Dress

Cut 1 piece of ribbon 13 in. [33 cm] long and thread through sps at neck edge and secure.

Cut 2 pieces of ribbon 11 in. [28 cm] long and thread through sps at yoke on Back and Front and secure.

Sew 2 buttons in position on yoke having top button on neck edging and second button at end of 3rd row. (Using sp between 2nd and 3rd st on opposite side as buttonhole.)

Coat

Cut 1 piece of ribbon 13 in. [33 cm] long and thread through sps at neck edge and secure.

Cut 1 piece of ribbon 11 in. [28 cm] long and thread through sps at yoke on back and secure.

Cut 2 pieces of ribbon 6 in. [15 cm] long and thread through sps at yoke on each Front and secure.

Sew 3 buttons in position on yoke having top button on neck edging, second button at end of 3rd row and last button on 1st row of skirt.

Cushion cover

Materials

4 oz Coats *Cadenza Courtelle* Double Knitting main colour
3 oz contrasting colour
Milward Disc crochet hook 4·50 (no. 7)
OR
4 oz Coats *Carefree Bri-Nylon* Double Knitting main colour
3 oz contrasting colour
Milward Disc crochet hook 5·00 (no. 6)
Cushion pad 12 × 18 in. [31 × 46 cm]

Measurement

Finished size of cushion $11\frac{1}{2} \times 17\frac{1}{2}$ in. [29 × 45 cm]

Tension

First 5 pattern rows to $2\frac{1}{4}$ in. [56 mm].

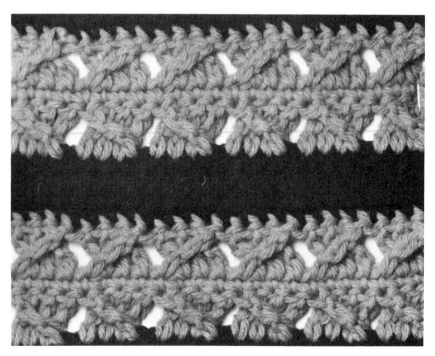

Front

Using 4·50 (no. 7) hook for *Cadenza*, 5·00 (no. 6) hook for *Carefree* and M, commence with 54 ch.

1st row 1 tr into 4th ch from hook, 1 tr into each ch, 1 ch, turn.

2nd row 1 dc into each tr, 1 dc into next ch. Fasten off M.

3rd row Attach C to last dc worked, 4 ch, 1 dbl tr into next dc, miss 3 dc, 1 dbl tr into next dc, * keeping yarn to front of last dbl tr work 1 dbl tr into each of 3 dc missed, miss next 3 free dc, 1 dbl tr into next dc; repeat from * ending with 1 dbl tr into each of next 2 dc, 1 ch, turn.

4th row As 2nd row ending with 4 ch, turn. Do not fasten off.

5th row Miss first dc, 1 dbl tr into next dc, * miss next dc, 1 dbl tr into each of next 3 dc, keeping yarn behind 3 dbl tr work 1 dbl tr into dc missed; repeat from * ending with 1 dbl tr into each of next 2 dc. Fasten off C.

6th row Attach M to last dbl tr worked, 1 dc into same place as join, 1 dc into each dbl tr, 1 dc into next ch, 3 ch, turn.

7th row Miss first dc, 1 tr into each dc, 1 ch, turn.

2nd to 7th row forms pattern.
Continue in pattern until work measures 17 in. [43 cm] approximately, ending with a 2nd pattern row. Fasten off.

Back

Using 4·50 (no. 7) hook for *Cadenza*, 5·00 (no. 6) hook for *Carefree* and M, commence with 54 ch.

1st row As 1st row of Front.

2nd row As 2nd of Front, ending with 3 ch, turn. Do not fasten off.

3rd row Miss first dc, 1 tr into each dc, 1 ch, turn.

Repeat last 2 rows until work measures 17 in. [43 cm] approximately. Fasten off.

To make up

Do not press. Place Back and Front right sides facing and with M oversew together leaving a 10 in. [25 cm] opening at one short end. Using 6 lengths of C 180 in. [457 cm] long make a twisted cord of approximately 60 in. [153 cm] in length. Sew cord along seam and top side of opening. Insert pad and slip stitch opening.

125

Motif bedspread

Materials

30 oz Coats *Carefree Bri-Nylon* Double Knitting main colour
20 oz first contrasting colour
22 oz second contrasting colour
Milward Disc crochet hook 5·00 (no. 6)

The above quantity is sufficient for a single size bed

Measurements

Size of motif 6 in. [152 mm]
Finished size 100 in. × 70 in. [254 × 178 cm] including edging

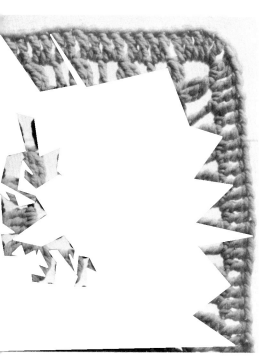

Tension

First 2 rows to 3½ in. [89 cm]. If your crochet is loose use a size finer hook, if tight use a size larger hook.

First motif

Using M commence with 6 ch, join with a ss to form a ring.

1st row 4 ch, leaving the last lp of each on hook work 2 dbl tr into ring, yarn over and draw through all lps on hook—a 2 dbl tr cl made, * 5 ch, a 3 dbl tr cl into ring; repeat from * twice more, 5 ch, 1 ss into first cl. Fasten off M.

2nd row Attach C to same place as ss, 4 ch, into same place as join work a 2 dbl tr cl 5 ch and a 3 dbl tr cl, * 3 ch, a 3 dbl tr cl into next lp, 3 ch, into next cl work a 3 dbl tr cl 5 ch and a 3 dbl tr cl; repeat from * twice more, 3 ch, a 3 dbl tr cl into next lp, 3 ch, 1 ss into first cl. Fasten off C.

3rd row Attach SC to next lp, 4 ch, into same lp work a 2 dbl tr cl and (3 ch, a 3 dbl tr cl) twice, * (3 ch, a 3 dbl tr cl into next lp) twice, 3 ch, into next lp work a 3 dbl tr cl and (3 ch, a 3 dbl tr cl) twice; repeat from * twice more, (3 ch, a 3 dbl tr cl into next lp) twice, 3 ch, 1 ss into first cl. Fasten off SC.

4th row Attach M to same place as last ss, 3 ch, * 3 tr into next lp, 3 tr into next cl corner, (3 tr into next lp, 1 tr into next cl) 4 times; repeat from * 3 times more omitting 1 tr at end of last repeat, 1 ss into 3rd of 3 ch. Fasten off M.

Second motif

Work as First motif for 3 rows.

4th row Attach M to same place as last ss, 3 ch, 3 tr into next lp, 2 tr into next cl, 1 ss into centre tr on any corner of first motif, 1 tr into same place as last tr on second motif, * 1 tr into next lp on second motif, 1 ss into corresponding tr on first motif, 2 tr into same lp on second motif, 1 ss into corresponding tr on first motif, 1 tr into next cl on second motif; repeat from * 4 times more, 1 tr into same cl on second motif, 1 ss into corresponding tr of next corner on first motif, 1 tr into same place as last tr on second motif and complete as first motif. Fasten off.

Make 16 rows of 11 motifs joining adjacent sides as second motif was joined to first. Where four corners meet join 3rd and 4th motifs to previous joining.

Edging

1st row Attach M to centre tr of 3 tr group at any corner, 4 ch, into same place as join work a 2 dbl tr cl 5 ch and a 3 dbl tr cl, 2 ch, miss 2 tr, 1 dbl tr into next st, 2 ch, miss next st, a 3 dbl tr cl into next st, 2 ch, miss next st, 1 dbl tr into next st and continue in this manner all round working a 3 dbl tr cl 5 ch and a 3 dbl tr cl into centre tr of 3 tr group at each corner, ending with 1 ss into first cl.

2nd row 1 ss into corner lp, 4 ch, 6 dbl tr into same lp, 2 dbl tr into each 2 ch lp and 7 dbl tr into each corner lp, ending with 1 ss into 4th of 4 ch. Fasten off.

Do not press.